MILITARY AND VETERAN ISSUES

AF757746

SERVICEMEMBERS SEPARATED FOR NON-DISABILITY MENTAL CONDITIONS

A REVIEW

MILITARY AND VETERAN ISSUES

Additional books in this series can be found on Nova's website under the Series tab.

Additional e-books in this series can be found on Nova's website under the e-book tab.

MILITARY AND VETERAN ISSUES

SERVICEMEMBERS SEPARATED FOR NON-DISABILITY MENTAL CONDITIONS

A REVIEW

SCOTT NORTON
EDITOR

NOVINKA

New York

NOTICE TO THE READER

Library of Congress Cataloging-in-Publication Data

ISBN: 978-1-63483-078-2

Published by Nova Science Publishers, Inc. † New York

CONTENTS

Preface		**vii**
Chapter 1	Defense Health Care: Better Tracking and Oversight Needed of Servicemember Separations for Non-Disability Mental Conditions *United States Government Accountability Office*	**1**
Chapter 2	Defense Health Care: Additional Efforts Needed to Ensure Compliance with Personality Disorder Separation Requirements *United States Government Accountability Office*	**31**
Index		**61**

PREFACE

Non-disability mental conditions, such as personality disorders, can render a servicemember unsuitable for military service and can lead to an administrative separation. This book examines the extent to which the Department of Defense (DOD) and the military services are able to identify the number of enlisted servicemembers separated for non-disability mental conditions, and the military services are complying with DOD requirements when separating enlisted servicemembers for non-disability mental conditions, including personality disorders, and how DOD and the military services oversee such separations.

In: Service Members Separated ...
Editor: Scott Norton

ISBN: 978-1-63483-078-2

Chapter 1

DEFENSE HEALTH CARE: BETTER TRACKING AND OVERSIGHT NEEDED OF SERVICEMEMBER SEPARATIONS FOR NON-DISABILITY MENTAL CONDITIONS*

United States Government Accountability Office

ABBREVIATIONS

DOD	Department of Defense
IDP	imminent danger pay
JAG	Judge Advocate General
PTSD	post-traumatic stress disorder
NDAA	National Defense Authorization Act
VA	Department of Veterans Affairs

* This is an edited, reformatted and augmented version of The United States Government Accountability Office publication, GAO-15-266, dated February 2015.

WHY GAO DID THIS STUDY

Non-disability mental conditions, such as personality disorders, can render a servicemember unsuitable for military service and can lead to an administrative separation. GAO was mandated to report on non-disability mental condition separations. This report examines the extent to which DOD and the military services are able to identify the number of enlisted servicemembers separated for non-disability mental conditions, and the military services are complying with DOD requirements when separating enlisted servicemembers for non-disability mental conditions, including personality disorders, and how DOD and the military services oversee such separations. GAO analyzed DOD and the military services' separation policies, policies related to tracking separations, reports the military services submitted to DOD regarding compliance with separation requirements, and interviewed DOD and military service officials.

WHAT GAO RECOMMENDS

GAO recommends that DOD and the military services develop a method to identify the number of servicemembers separated for non-disability mental conditions and take a number of actions to ensure that their policies and processes can ensure that servicemembers are appropriately separated for non-disability mental conditions in accordance with DOD's separation requirements. DOD generally concurred with GAO's recommendations, but did not provide information on how or when it plans to implement the recommendations.

WHAT GAO FOUND

The Department of Defense (DOD) and three of the four military services—Army, Navy, and Marine Corps—cannot identify the number of enlisted servicemembers separated for non-disability mental conditions—mental conditions that are not considered service-related disabilities. For most non-disability mental condition separations, these services use the broad separation code, "condition, not a disability," which mixes non-disability mental conditions with non-disability physical conditions, such as obesity, making it difficult to distinguish one type of condition from the other. In contrast, the Air Force is able to identify such servicemembers because it uses all five of the separation codes specific to non-disability mental conditions. DOD policy requires the military services to use a separation code so that DOD can track and analyze separations. Moreover, federal standards for internal control state that all transactions need to be clearly and accurately documented and readily available for examination when needed. The three services had varying reasons as to why they use the broad separation code. For example, Army officials believed that stating in servicemembers' discharge papers that they were discharged for non-disability mental conditions might stigmatize them with future employers. However, DOD stated that there are ways to protect servicemembers in this regard by providing them with discharge papers that are more general and that do not disclose specific reasons for discharge. By not systematically identifying or periodically evaluating the number of separations for non-disability mental conditions, DOD and the services cannot assess how well the separation policy and process are working or inform key stakeholders, including the Congress, about separation frequency, trends, and other data.

The military services lack separation policies that address all of DOD's eight requirements for separating servicemembers with non-disability mental conditions; both DOD and the services also lack oversight over such separations. From fiscal years 2008 through 2012, DOD required the services to report on their compliance with DOD requirements for personality disorder separations, one of the non-disability mental conditions. Most of the services reported by fiscal year 2012 that they were not compliant with all eight requirements and many of the 20 reports contained incomplete and inconsistent information. For example, 19 reports were missing information on reserve members. DOD discontinued these reports and did not institute any other oversight, which is inconsistent with the internal control standard for monitoring. GAO also found, based on a review of the services' separation policies, that the services have not updated their policies to meet all DOD requirements for non-disability mental condition separations. For example, Navy officials stated that they were unaware that DOD separation policies had changed since 2008 until GAO's review. DOD officials stated that the military services are responsible for conducting oversight of their separation processes; however, GAO found that the military services do not have processes to oversee non-disability mental condition separations. Without up-to-date and consistent policies and oversight processes, DOD and the military services cannot ensure that servicemembers separated for non-disability mental conditions have been afforded the protections intended by DOD's separation requirements and that servicemembers have been appropriately separated for such conditions.

* * *

February 13, 2015

The Honorable John McCain
Chairman

The Honorable Jack Reed
Ranking Member
Committee on Armed Services United States Senate

The Honorable Mac Thornberry
Chairman

The Honorable Adam Smith
Ranking Member
Committee on Armed Services House of Representatives

The Department of Defense (DOD) requires that all servicemembers be physically and psychologically suitable for military service. DOD policy permits an enlisted servicemember to be involuntarily separated from the military if the servicemember's mental condition is severe enough that it interferes with the servicemember's ability to function in the military.[1] Servicemembers diagnosed with a mental condition may be eligible to receive disability compensation benefits from the Department of Veterans Affairs (VA) if the mental condition was incurred or aggravated while the servicemember was on active duty, such as developing post-traumatic stress disorder (PTSD) related to combat. However, if the mental condition is not incurred or aggravated while on active duty, it is not considered a service-related disability by DOD and VA; in other words, it is considered a non-disability mental condition.

Servicemember separations from the military for non-disability mental conditions are processed as administrative separations, and DOD has requirements that the military services—Army, Air Force, Navy, and Marine Corps—must follow when processing these separations.[2] DOD's current processing requirements apply to separations for all non-disability mental conditions;[3] however, prior to 2011, most of the department's requirements only applied to separations for one type of non-disability mental condition—personality disorder, which is defined as a longstanding, inflexible pattern of behavior that deviates markedly from expected behavior, has an onset in adolescence or early adulthood, and leads to distress or impairment.

In 2008, we conducted a review of records of enlisted servicemembers who had served in Operation Enduring Freedom or Operation Iraqi Freedom and had been separated from the military because of a personality disorder. [4] We found that DOD and the military services did not have adequate oversight to ensure that separation requirements were being adhered to when servicemembers were separated for personality disorders. We made recommendations to improve DOD's and the military services' oversight of such separations. As a result of our review, in January 2009, DOD required the military services to annually review a sample of personality disorder separations to determine whether DOD separation requirements were being followed and to report the results to DOD.

The National Defense Authorization Act (NDAA) for Fiscal Year 2014 mandated GAO to examine issues regarding separations of servicemembers for non-disability mental conditions. For our review, we examined (1) the extent to which DOD and the military services are able to identify the number of enlisted servicemembers separated for non-disability mental conditions, and (2) the extent to which the military services are complying with DOD requirements when separating enlisted servicemembers for non-disability mental conditions, including personality disorders, and how DOD and the military services oversee such separations. The NDAA also mandated GAO to report on the ability of servicemembers administratively separated for a non-disability mental condition to receive VA health benefits, which is addressed in appendix I.

To analyze the extent to which DOD and the military services are able to identify the number of enlisted servicemembers that were administratively separated because of a non-disability mental condition, we reviewed DOD and the military services documents, such as DOD's policy on the use of codes to track specific types of separations,[5] and interviewed DOD and military service officials to understand the type of tracking conducted and data maintained on separations for non-disability mental conditions, and any requirements related to tracking such separations. Our review of documents and interviews allowed us to determine the type of information that DOD and the military services have available to identify servicemembers separated because of non-disability mental conditions. We assessed this information against DOD policy—which requires separation codes to be used by the military services so that DOD can track and analyze separations by their cause, as well as against the federal internal control standards. The federal internal control standards require agencies to have control activities that help ensure management's directives are carried out.[6] For example, management should have a control that all transactions—such as the separations of enlisted servicemembers—are clearly documented and the documentation should be available for examination.

To determine the extent to which the military services are complying with DOD requirements when separating enlisted servicemembers for non-disability mental conditions, including personality disorders, and how DOD and the military services oversee such separations, we reviewed DOD's and the military services' separation policies to identify requirements for separating servicemembers for non-disability mental conditions, how these requirements evolved since our last review in 2008, and whether the requirements have been consistent between DOD and each of the military services' policies. We also interviewed DOD and military service officials to understand the services' administrative separation processes for non-disability mental conditions and any oversight conducted by DOD or the military services to ensure the processes in place are effective in ensuring DOD separation requirements are met. Lastly, we reviewed and analyzed annual reports the military services submitted to DOD from fiscal year 2008 through fiscal year 2012 on their compliance with DOD's separation requirements when separating servicemembers for a personality disorder. Our interviews and review of policies and compliance reports allowed us to determine the practices that DOD and the military services use to oversee separations of enlisted servicemembers for a personality disorder or other non-disability mental conditions. We assessed the information we collected against DOD's separation policy. In addition, we assessed the information against the federal internal control standard for monitoring, which states that there should be reasonable assurance that ongoing monitoring occurs in the course of normal operations.[7] The standard also states that, when deficiencies have been identified, there should be a process to resolve them; and that the resolution process is not complete until action has been taken to correct deficiencies, produce improvements, or demonstrate that findings and recommendations do not warrant management action.

We conducted this performance audit from April 2014 to February 2015 in accordance with generally accepted government auditing standards. Those standards require that we plan and perform the audit to obtain sufficient, appropriate evidence to provide a reasonable basis for our findings and conclusions based on our audit objectives. We believe that the evidence obtained provides a reasonable basis for our findings and conclusions based on our audit objectives.

BACKGROUND

Military Services' Separation Process

Enlisted servicemembers can be separated from the military when they are found to be unsuitable for continued military service. If a servicemember is diagnosed with a non-disability mental condition that interferes with the servicemember's ability to function in the military, a commanding officer may initiate the separation process. Separated servicemembers may appeal their separation to a discharge review board within 15 years after separation from the military. Further, separated servicemembers may appeal the discharge review board's decision by applying to a board for the correction of military records.[8]

Separation Documentation

Once enlisted servicemembers have been separated from military service, they receive a certificate of release from the military— Department of Defense Form 214 (DD Form 214)—that includes dates of service, last duty assignment, pay grade and rank, awards received, and a characterization of their service—such as honorable or general under honorable conditions.[9] Copies of the DD Form 214 are sent to various entities, such as the applicable military service, VA, and the servicemember. Servicemembers receive two copies of the DD Form 214—a copy that includes the characterization of their service and the reason for the separation and one that does not. The reason for the separation is noted by a separation code, as well as a narrative that explains the reason for the separation.

Separation Codes

According to DOD policy, separation codes are to be used by the military services so that data on the cause of separations can be collected and trends in separations analyzed, which may, in turn, influence changes in DOD separation policy. DOD established six separation codes that the military services may use for non-disability mental conditions on the DD Form 214, but the military services have discretion as to which codes they choose to use.[10] Five of these separation codes pertain only to non-disability mental conditions. They are (1) acute adjustment disorder, (2) disruptive behavior disorder, (3) impulse control disorder, (4) personality disorder, and (5) other non-disability mental disorder.[11] The sixth code available for use by the military services, "condition, not a disability," is a broader separation code that includes both non-disability physical and mental conditions.[12]

DOD's Separation Requirements

DOD's separation policy, dated January 27, 2014, contains eight separation requirements that the military services must follow when separating enlisted servicemembers for non-disability mental conditions.[13] Of the eight separation requirements, five apply to all enlisted servicemembers and three more apply only to enlisted servicemembers who served in an imminent danger pay (IDP) area, such as Iraq or Afghanistan.[14]

1. The servicemember must be notified in writing that a non-disability mental condition is the basis of the proposed separation,
2. the servicemember must be formally counseled concerning deficiencies and afforded an opportunity to overcome those deficiencies,
3. evidence must demonstrate that the servicemember is unable to function effectively because of a non-disability mental condition,
4. the servicemember must receive a non-disability mental condition diagnosis by a authorized mental health provider,15 and
5. the servicemember must be counseled in writing that the diagnosis of a non-disability mental condition does not qualify as a disability.
6. For servicemembers who served in an IDP area, the non-disability mental condition diagnosis must
7. be corroborated by a peer- or higher-level mental health professional,

8. be endorsed by the military service's surgeon general, and
9. include an assessment to determine whether the servicemember has symptoms of PTSD or other mental illness co-morbidity.

Over time, DOD has expanded its separation requirements. In 2011 and 2014 DOD revised its policy by extending its separation requirements to apply to servicemembers being separated for any non-disability mental condition. See table 1 for an explanation of the policy changes since 2008.

Table 1. Changes to Department of Defense (DOD) Separation Requirements for Non-Disability Mental Conditions, August 2008 to January 2014

DOD requirements as of August 28, 2008	DOD requirements as of September 30, 2011	DOD requirements as of January 27, 2014
Servicemember must be notified in writing of the basis of the proposed separation.	No change	No change
Servicemember must be formally counseled concerning deficiencies and afforded an opportunity to overcome those deficiencies.	No change	No change
Evidence must demonstrate that the servicemember is unable to function effectively because of a *personality disorder*.	No change	Requirement expanded to include *other non-disability mental conditions*.
Servicemember must receive a *personality disorder diagnosis* by a psychiatrist or PhD-level psychologist who determines that the personality disorder interferes with the servicemember's ability to function in the military.	No change	Requirement expanded to include *other non-disability mental conditions*, and diagnosis may be made by an authorized mental health provider who determines that the disorder interferes with the servicemember's ability to function in the military.[b]
Servicemember must be counseled in writing that *the diagnosis of a personality disorder* does not qualify as a disability.	No change	Requirement expanded to include *other non-disability mental conditions*.
Additional requirements that apply to enlisted servicemembers who have served or are currently serving in imminent danger pay areas:[a]		

Table 1. (Continued)

DOD requirements as of August 28, 2008	DOD requirements as of September 30, 2011	DOD requirements as of January 27, 2014
A personality disorder diagnosis must be corroborated by a peer- or higher-level mental health professional.	Requirement expanded to include other non-disability mental conditions.	No change
A personality disorder diagnosis must be endorsed by the surgeon general of the military service concerned.	Requirement expanded to include other non-disability mental conditions.	No change
A personality disorder diagnosis must address post-traumatic stress disorder or other mental illness co-morbidity.	Requirement expanded to include other non-disability mental conditions.	No change

Source: GAO analysis of DOD policy. | GAO-15-266.

Notes: The separation requirements are based on DOD Instruction 1332.14 Enlisted Administrative Separations. Underlined and bolded text indicates the requirement in the August 2008 version of the instruction that applies to a personality disorder diagnosis only and the text in the subsequent versions of the instruction that expands the requirement to apply to all non-disability mental conditions.

[a] Servicemembers receive imminent danger pay (IDP) when they are on duty outside of the United States and are subject to the threat of physical harm or imminent danger due to wartime conditions, terrorism, civil insurrection, or civil war. In some locations, IDP applies only for duty on the ground; and in other locations, ground, airspace, or duty aboard a ship at sea qualify.

[b] Based on DOD policy, an authorized mental health provider is a psychiatrist or clinical psychologist, a person with a doctorate in clinical social work, or a psychiatric nurse practitioner. In cases of outpatient mental health evaluations only, licensed clinical social workers who possess a master's degree in clinical social work will also be considered authorized mental health providers.

DOD and Three of the Four Military Services Cannot Identify the Number of Enlisted Servicemembers Separated for Non-Disability Mental Conditions

DOD and three of the four military services—Army, Navy, and Marine Corps—cannot identify the number of enlisted servicemembers separated for non-disability mental conditions because, for most separations, they do not use available codes to specifically designate the reason why servicemembers were separated. Instead, they use the broad separation code, "condition, not a disability," that mixes non-disability mental conditions with non-disability physical conditions, making it difficult to distinguish one from the other without a time-consuming and resource-intensive record review. In contrast, the Air Force is able to track the specific reasons for its servicemember separations because it uses the full array of separation codes available.

DOD policy requires a separation code to be used by the military services so that DOD can track and analyze the reason for separations and evaluate DOD's separation policy to determine if changes are needed. However, according to DOD officials, the military services can choose to use any of the six available codes that DOD provides the military services to record non-disability mental conditions, including the "condition, not a disability" code. Moreover, under the internal control standard for control activities, all transactions—such as separations of enlisted servicemembers—need to be clearly and accurately documented so they can be examined when needed; for example, to monitor trends in the reasons for servicemembers' separations.[16]

The three military services had varying reasons for using the broad separation code, "condition, not a disability." Navy and Marine Corps officials stated that they have historically used this code for most separations but Navy officials could not explain why they use this broad code instead of using one of the separation codes specific to non-disability mental conditions. Marine Corps officials cited concerns with potential stigma the servicemember may face if a more specific code is used. Army officials had a similar concern, stating that they use the broad separation code for most non-disability mental condition separations to protect enlisted servicemembers after they leave the service. Army and Marine Corps officials told us they were concerned that employers may request the servicemember's copy of the DD Form 214 that has the separation code on it, and having a code specific to a mental condition might stigmatize the servicemember. Army officials stated that this issue has been discussed in media articles for several years.[17]

In contrast, both Air Force and DOD officials told us that they do not have evidence that including the separation code on the DD Form 214 has caused problems for servicemembers, as suggested by the Army. An Air Force official said that, unlike the Army, the Air Force does not have information that using these codes has caused problems for separated Air Force servicemembers. Likewise, DOD officials told us that they have not heard that this is a problem. According to DOD officials, characterization of service, such as honorable or dishonorable, is usually the piece of information that employers want from the form. By including the characterization of service on both of the servicemember's copies of the DD Form 214, DOD believes that the servicemember could provide an employer with the copy that does not contain the reason for the separation and the employer will be satisfied because the characterization of service is indicated.[18]

Because the three military services are using the broad separation code "condition, not a disability" for most separations, the resulting data cannot be used to identify the number of servicemembers separated for non-disability mental conditions. There is no other systematic way to track these separations; that is, without a tedious and time-consuming manual review. In one instance for example, in response to a request from DOD for information on the number of separations for non-disability mental conditions, the Army undertook a 6-month manual review of over 2,000 servicemember files—all because it does not delineate separations for non-disability mental versus non-disability physical conditions in any data system. If DOD and the military services cannot systematically identify or periodically evaluate the number of enlisted servicemembers separated for non-disability mental conditions, they cannot assess how well the separation policy and process is working or respond specifically to key stakeholders, including the Congress, about trends in or concerns about separations for non-disability mental conditions.

Military Services' Separation Policies Do Not Address All DOD Requirements for Non-Disability Mental Conditions Separations, and DOD and the Services Lack Oversight of Such Separations

From fiscal years 2008 through 2012, when the services were filing compliance reports, most services did not report full compliance with DOD separation requirements for separations for personality disorder. We also found that the reports contained incomplete and inconsistent data, and DOD conducted limited review of these reports. Further, based on a review of separation policies, we found that none of the services' policies address all DOD requirements for non-disability mental condition separations. Additionally, DOD and the military services do not have oversight processes in place to ensure compliance with DOD requirements in this regard.

Most Services Did Not Report Full Compliance with Requirements for Personality Disorder Separations, the Reports Contained Incomplete and Inconsistent Data, and DOD Conducted Limited Review

Most of the Military Services Had Not Reported Full Compliance When DOD Discontinued the Compliance Reports

From fiscal years 2008 through 2012, DOD required the military services to monitor and report to DOD on their compliance with DOD requirements for separating servicemembers for personality disorders; however, while the services generally reported improved compliance over the 5 years of reporting, we found in the 2012 compliance reports that three of the services had not yet achieved full compliance with all of DOD's 2008 separation requirements. For each of the 20 compliance reports the services submitted for fiscal years 2008 through 2012, the military services were required to review a sample of at least 10 percent of their personality disorder separations for the fiscal year and assess the service's compliance with DOD's 2008 separation requirements. Compliance, according to DOD, was achieved if the sample reviewed met a 90 percent compliance threshold for each requirement. According to DOD officials, the annual compliance reports were discontinued in 2013 because the military services' 2012 compliance reports indicated that the services were compliant with all of DOD's 2008 requirements. However, it is unclear how DOD came to this conclusion when our review of the 2012 compliance reports found that the Air Force, Marine Corps, and Navy did not report compliance with all DOD requirements. Specifically, the Marine Corps reported compliance below 90 percent with one requirement and the Air Force was below this compliance rate for two requirements.[19] Further, the Navy did not report on its compliance with three of the eight separation requirements, so DOD could not have known the Navy's level of compliance in those areas.[20]

Among the 20 compliance reports submitted during fiscal years 2008 through 2012, the services reported the most difficulty meeting the requirement to notify all servicemembers that a personality disorder diagnosis does not constitute a disability. For example, the Marine Corps reported 78 percent or less compliance with this requirement in 3 of its 5 reports.[21] In the Air Force's fiscal year 2009 compliance report, after finding itself noncompliant with this DOD requirement, the Air Force acknowledged that its policy incorrectly stated that servicemember notification was only required for servicemembers who served in an IDP area. However, even after the Air Force updated its policy in September 2010 and made a correction in this regard, the

Air Force's compliance with this requirement was 81 percent in fiscal year 2011 and 89 percent in fiscal year 2012. Because three of the four services were noncompliant with at least one requirement in their 2012 reports, DOD's discontinuation of these reports was premature. The federal internal control standard for monitoring states that there should be reasonable assurance that ongoing monitoring occurs in the course of normal operations. Further, it requires reasonable assurance that deficiencies are identified and corrected or otherwise resolved.[22]

Many Compliance Reports Were Incomplete or Contained Inconsistent Information

Our review of the services' compliance reports found examples of incomplete and inconsistent information in many of the 20 compliance reports submitted by the military services to DOD between fiscal years 2008 and 2012. Regarding incomplete information in the compliance reports, we found three areas of concern:

- *Compliance information for reservists and National Guard members was missing.* Nineteen of the 20 compliance reports did not assess compliance with separation requirements for reservists and National Guard members who were separated while not on active duty.[23] Some military service officials stated that they did not provide information on these reservists and National Guard members because DOD did not specifically ask for them to be included in the reports. However, DOD instructed the Secretaries of the Army, the Air Force, and the Navy and the Commandant of the Marine Corps to include a random sampling of all personality disorder separations for each military department, in which reservists and National Guard members are included as part of their respective departments.
- *Compliance information for servicemembers who served in an IDP area was missing.* Eight of the 20 compliance reports did not indicate how many of the servicemembers in their review sample had served in an IDP area, if any. [24] As a result, it is not clear the extent to which compliance was assessed in these reports for the three separation requirements that apply only to servicemembers who served in an IDP area. Further, in its fiscal year 2011 report, Navy reported that its review sample did not include any servicemembers who served in an IDP area. Therefore, Navy could not have assessed compliance with the three separation requirements that apply to these servicemembers,

even though Navy reported 100 percent compliance with them. While DOD did not explicitly state that servicemembers that served in an IDP area should be included in the sample reviewed by the military services, three of the eight separation requirements only apply to such servicemembers, so the need to include these types of servicemembers in the review sample in order for DOD to gauge compliance should have been clear.

- *The Navy had incomplete information in its fiscal year 2010 compliance report.* The Navy failed to complete the reporting requirement for its fiscal year 2010 compliance report because its findings were based on a 4 percent sample of the total number of servicemembers separated for a personality disorder in that fiscal year—not the 10 percent required by DOD. In its compliance report, Navy stated that additional separations would be reviewed to fulfill DOD's sample size requirement, but according to DOD and Navy officials, the results of this review were never reported to DOD. When asked about these additional reviews, Navy officials could not offer an explanation regarding whether the reviews were conducted.

In addition to incomplete information in the compliance reports, we found that two of the four services—Army and Navy—reported inconsistent numbers in several of their compliance reports. Specifically, DOD required the services to include in each annual compliance report the total number of personality disorder separations. However, the Army's and the Navy's reports of these numbers were not consistent across the 5 years, as demonstrated in table 2. According to DOD officials, DOD could not find documentation of follow-up with the services regarding these inconsistencies.[25]

DOD's Review of the Military Services' Compliance Reports for Personality Disorder Separations Was Limited

Based on interviews with officials from DOD and the military services, we found that almost no follow-up was conducted by DOD with the military services regarding the compliance reports even though the services reported noncompliance with separation requirements across the 5 years of reports. DOD officials stated that they received the annual compliance reports from the military services and assumed that the information provided in these reports was accurate, given that they were signed by each of the three military service secretaries and a representative of the Commandant of the Marine Corps.

By not reviewing the information provided, DOD did not know that the reports contained inconsistent and incomplete information, and the agency made the decision to end the compliance reports based on what we found to be faulty assurances of compliance. To discontinue compliance reporting and not institute any other type of oversight is inconsistent with the standards for internal control in the federal government, which states that there should generally be assurance that ongoing monitoring occurs in the course of normal operations.[26]

Table 2. Examples of Inconsistent Data Reported in the Army and the Navy Annual Compliance Reports on Separations of Servicemembers for Personality Disorders

Army	Navy
Example 1: The Army reported in its fiscal year 2008 report that there were *567* separations in that year. •In its fiscal year 2010 report, the Army stated there were *641* separations in fiscal year 2008.	*Example 1*: The Navy reported in its fiscal year 2008 report that there were *946* separations in that year. •In its fiscal year 2010 report, the Navy stated there were *1086* separations in fiscal year 2008. •In its fiscal year 2012 report, the Navy stated there were *975*separations in fiscal year 2008.
Example 2: The Army reported in its fiscal year 2009 report that there were *255* separations in that year. •In its fiscal year 2010 report, the Army stated there were *575* separations in fiscal year 2009.	*Example 2*: The Navy reported in its fiscal year 2011 report that there were 189 separations in that year. •In its fiscal year 2012 report, the Navy stated there were *173* separations in fiscal year 2011.

Source: GAO analysis of Department of Defense data. | GAO-15-266.

The Military Services' Policies Have Not Been Updated to Fully Address DOD Requirements for Separating Servicemembers for All Non-Disability Mental Conditions

In addition to problems we identified with compliance reports focusing on personality disorder separations, we also found that the Army, the Navy, the Marine Corps, and components of the Air Force—namely, the Reserves and National Guard—have been separating servicemembers for non-disability mental conditions according to policies that are not consistent with all DOD requirements.27 Each of the services has policies for separating servicemembers for non-disability mental conditions; however, we found these policies to be inconsistent with DOD policy because they have not been updated to include all of the changes in DOD requirements over time. Specifically, we found the following.

- The Army active duty separation policy is not consistent with one of DOD's separation requirements. [28] Specifically, one requirement has not been expanded to apply to servicemembers separated for all non-disability mental conditions.[29] In addition, the Army Reserves and National Guard separation policy was updated in March 2014 yet does not contain all of DOD's separation requirements, such as the requirement that servicemembers be counseled in writing that their diagnosis does not qualify as a disability.[30]
- The Navy's separation policy has not been updated to be fully consistent with DOD policy.[31] The Navy officials stated they were unaware that DOD had revised its separation policy in 2011, and again in 2014, until we discussed this with them in May 2014 during the course of our review.
- The Marine Corps' separation policy has not been updated to be fully consistent with DOD policy, since the Navy is responsible for revising and implementing such policies for the Marine Corps.[32]
- The Air Force Reserves and National Guard separation policy was created in 2005 and has not been updated over time as DOD has updated its separation requirements for non-disability mental conditions.[33] For example, the policy does not contain the separation requirements applicable to servicemembers who served in an IDP area.

Because the services have been separating servicemembers based on outdated DOD policy, some servicemembers may not have been afforded the protections intended by DOD's updated separation requirements. For example, servicemembers who served in an IDP area may not have had their diagnosis endorsed by the military services' Office of the Surgeon General as required by DOD and have been separated without the benefit of a confirmation of their diagnosis by this senior medical entity.

During the course of our review, we also found that the Air Force National Guard does not have a process to separate National Guard members for non-disability mental conditions. In 2013, Air Force National Guard reported that it had not been separating Guard members for non-disability mental conditions because it did not have a process to get a mental health assessment or diagnosis for National Guard members. National Guard members believed to have non-disability mental conditions were either returned to duty or separated for another reason such as misconduct or unsatisfactory performance of duty. According to DOD policy, when separation for unsatisfactory performance or misconduct is warranted, separating a servicemember for a non-disability mental condition is not appropriate.[34] Under federal internal control standards, control activities should be established to help ensure that performance is correctly assessed and transactions are accurately recorded.[35] Accordingly, there should be processes in place so that, if a servicemember is identified as potentially having a non-disability mental condition that affects the member's ability to perform military duties, that servicemember can be separated for such a condition in accordance with DOD requirements, if appropriate.

The Air Force developed a corrective action plan to address the National Guard's inability to separate National Guard members for non-disability mental conditions; however, this plan was never implemented. According to officials, the biggest challenge in implementing the plan was that the Air Force National Guard does not have authorized mental health providers who can diagnose non-disability mental conditions. Without a mental condition diagnosis by an authorized mental health provider, a servicemember cannot be separated for a non-disability mental condition, according to Air Force policy.[36] According to officials, the Air Force National Guard would need to be tasked and provided related funding to have these providers available. The officials could not provide any further information on why no further action was taken to correct this identified problem. Further, Air Force officials stated that they could not identify the number of servicemembers potentially affected by this problem without conducting a comprehensive file review. Air Force National Guard members that are thought to have a non-disability mental condition but are separated for another reason, such as misconduct, risk not receiving the protections of DOD's separation requirements.

DOD and the Military Services Do Not Conduct Oversight for Servicemember Separations for Non-Disability Mental Conditions

Beyond the limited review DOD conducted of the military services' compliance reports conducted for personality disorder separations, which was discontinued after fiscal year 2012, DOD and military service officials stated they do not conduct any oversight of all non-disability mental condition separations. In September 2011, DOD revised its separation policy by expanding the three requirements that apply to servicemembers who served in an IDP area to include servicemembers separated for any non-disability mental conditions, not just for personality disorders.[37] In January 2014, DOD again revised this policy and expanded the separations requirements so that all eight requirements apply to servicemembers separated for any non-disability mental condition. However, DOD officials stated that they have not required the military services to conduct any review of their compliance with DOD's separation requirements for all non-disability mental conditions to determine whether they are being followed. As noted previously, the internal control standard for monitoring states that controls should be designed to assure that ongoing monitoring occurs in the course of normal operations.[38]

According to DOD officials, the military services are responsible for conducting oversight of their separation processes, not DOD. However, while some of the military services have review steps within their process for separating servicemembers for non-disability mental conditions, none of the services have an entity-wide oversight process, such as conducting an annual review, to oversee separations and provide reasonable assurance that the review steps they have in place are effective at ensuring DOD separation requirements are met. Specifically, we found their review processes are the following:

- The Air Force separation process includes reviews of separation packages—which is prepared by a commanding officer—by the Air Force central personnel office and a Judge Advocate General (JAG) Corps attorney prior to separation.[39] Officials from these offices told us that the purpose of the reviews is to ensure that the appropriate documentation is present to support the separation.[40]
- The Army's JAG Corps also reviews all separation packages prior to separation to ensure documentation is present and is consistent with law and policy, according to Army officials.[41] While this is the current

practice, Army officials also told us that they have plans in place to start conducting oversight of separations for non-disability mental conditions. Specifically, Army officials stated that separations for non-disability mental conditions will be included as part of the Army Organizational Inspection Program, which will review a sample of active duty servicemember separations at local commands to see if documentation is present that indicates that DOD separation requirements have been met. These inspections will not include reserve and National Guard member separations. Army officials stated they plan to conduct the first inspection in January 2015.[42]

- The Marine Corps Judge Advocates review the separation packages for personality disorder separations—but not for other non-disability mental conditions separations—to ensure documentation is present and is consistent with law and policy, according to Marine Corps officials.
- The Navy does not conduct any review of the separation package prepared by a commanding officer prior to the servicemember's separation.

The absence of a routine and comprehensive entity-wide oversight mechanism—such as an annual compliance review—prevents the military services from knowing if they are complying with all of DOD requirements and appropriately separating servicemembers with non-disability mental conditions.

CONCLUSION

The inability to easily identify the number of enlisted servicemembers separated for non-disability mental conditions hinders oversight by DOD and the military services to ensure that servicemembers are being separated appropriately. For example, without such data, DOD cannot determine how many separated servicemembers have served in IDP areas—who may be at greater risk of having a service-related mental condition, such as PTSD—or determine if these servicemembers have been afforded the protections intended by the separation requirements, such as ensuring they are assessed for service-related mental conditions prior to being separated for a non-disability mental condition. Further, lack of such data prevents DOD from being able to conduct analyses—such as trends in non-disability mental condition separations over time—that are important for determining whether the separation policy is working, and if not, how it should be changed.

Absent an effective process for monitoring and reporting compliance, DOD and the military services cannot assure that the military services are complying with DOD requirements for separating servicemembers with non-disability mental conditions. The fact that some military services were not aware of or had not yet aligned their policies or processes with updated DOD requirements for separating servicemembers with non-disability mental conditions is of particular concern. Because the services have been separating servicemembers based on outdated DOD policy, the military services may not have been affording all servicemembers with the protections that DOD intended through its recent updates of separation requirements for non-disability mental conditions. As a result, some servicemembers may have been separated for non-disability mental conditions inappropriately. It is also of concern that, although the Air Force reported its inability to separate National Guard members for non-disability mental conditions in 2013, it has made no progress in correcting this issue. Meanwhile, these members risk not receiving the protections intended by DOD's separation requirements.

RECOMMENDATIONS FOR EXECUTIVE ACTION

To improve identification of enlisted servicemembers separated for non-disability mental conditions, and to provide reasonable assurance that enlisted servicemembers, including Air Force National Guard members, are separated for non-disability mental conditions as appropriate and in accordance with DOD requirements, we recommend that the Secretary of Defense take the following six actions:

- Direct the Under Secretary of Defense for Personnel and Readiness and the Secretaries of the Army and the Navy and the Commandant of the Marine Corps to use the separation codes specific to a non-disability mental condition or develop another uniform method to track servicemembers who have been separated for specific non-disability mental conditions so that this information can be easily retrieved.
- Direct the Under Secretary of Defense for Personnel and Readiness and the Secretary of the Air Force to take steps to ensure there is an appropriately staffed process to identify and administratively separate

enlisted National Guard members who are unable to function effectively in the National Guard because of a non-disability mental condition.

- Direct the Secretaries of the Army, the Air Force, and the Navy and the Commandant of the Marine Corps to update their services' administrative separation policies to be consistent with DOD regulations for those servicemembers separated for all non-disability mental conditions.
- Direct the Secretaries of the Air Force and the Navy and the Commandant of the Marine Corps to implement processes to oversee separations for non-disability mental conditions, such as reinstituting the requirement of annual compliance reporting of a sample of administrative separations, using current DOD policy requirements as review criteria for servicemembers of all military services and their Reserve components.
- Direct the Secretary of the Army to ensure that Army's planned oversight of separations for non-disability mental conditions is implemented and incorporates reservists and National Guard members separated for such conditions, or that Army implement another process to oversee such administrative separations using current DOD policy requirements as review criteria for all servicemembers, including reservists and National Guard members.
- Direct the Under Secretary of Defense for Personnel and Readiness to review any processes used by the military services to oversee such administrative separations to ensure compliance with DOD requirements.

AGENCY COMMENTS AND OUR EVALUATION

We provided DOD and VA a draft of this report for advance review and comment. DOD generally concurred with our six recommendations. Regarding our recommendation that DOD direct the Secretaries and Commandant to use the existing separation codes specific to a non-disability mental condition or develop another uniform method to track such servicemember separations, DOD provided several reasons why it would not use the existing separation codes specific to non-disability mental conditions, including the possible stigmatization of the servicemember, but DOD agreed with the need to develop a method to uniformly track such separations. In its comments, DOD did not outline how it would develop a method to track these servicemember separations, nor when it would implement this or other of our recommendations. DOD and VA also provided technical comments, which we incorporated as appropriate.

Randall B. Williamson
Director,
Health Care

APPENDIX I: ELIGIBILITY OF SERVICEMEMBERS SEPARATED FOR NON-DISABILITY MENTAL CONDITIONS FOR VETERANS' HEALTH BENEFITS

Like any veteran separated from military service under other than dishonorable conditions, veterans separated for non-disability mental conditions are eligible to receive Department of Veterans Affairs (VA) health care benefits, if they meet certain service requirements.1 Generally, servicemembers must have served 24 continuous months, or the full period for which they were called or ordered to active duty, in order to be eligible to receive VA health care benefits.2

Once VA determines the eligibility of veterans who have applied for VA health care, it assigns them to an enrollment priority group.3 Generally, VA assigns veterans separated for non-disability mental conditions to priority groups 5 through 8.4 VA assigns the veterans as follows:

- *If the veteran has served in an imminent danger pay (IDP) area*: [5] the veteran is afforded what is known as enhanced enrollment status and is generally assigned to priority group 6.[6] The veteran is not subject to copayments for visits or medications for conditions potentially related to their service in an IDP area, such as physical injuries incurred while in service.[7] The veteran remains enrolled as priority group 6 for 5 years after discharge from the military. If during this 5-year, post-discharge period an eligibility status is gained that affords enrollment in a higher priority group, such as the finding of a compensable service-related medical condition, the veteran is immediately moved to the higher priority group. Once the 5-year term has ended, the veteran remains enrolled in the VA health care system but his priority for enrollment is reassessed and the veteran may be shifted to priority group 5, 7, or 8 depending on his household income.

- *If the veteran has not served in an IDP area*: the veteran is assigned to priority group 5, 7, or 8 based on income level. Veterans enrolled in these priority groups must agree to pay applicable copayments. Veterans remain enrolled in the VA health care system but are reassessed annually, and placed in a priority group based on the veteran's household income. (See fig. 1)

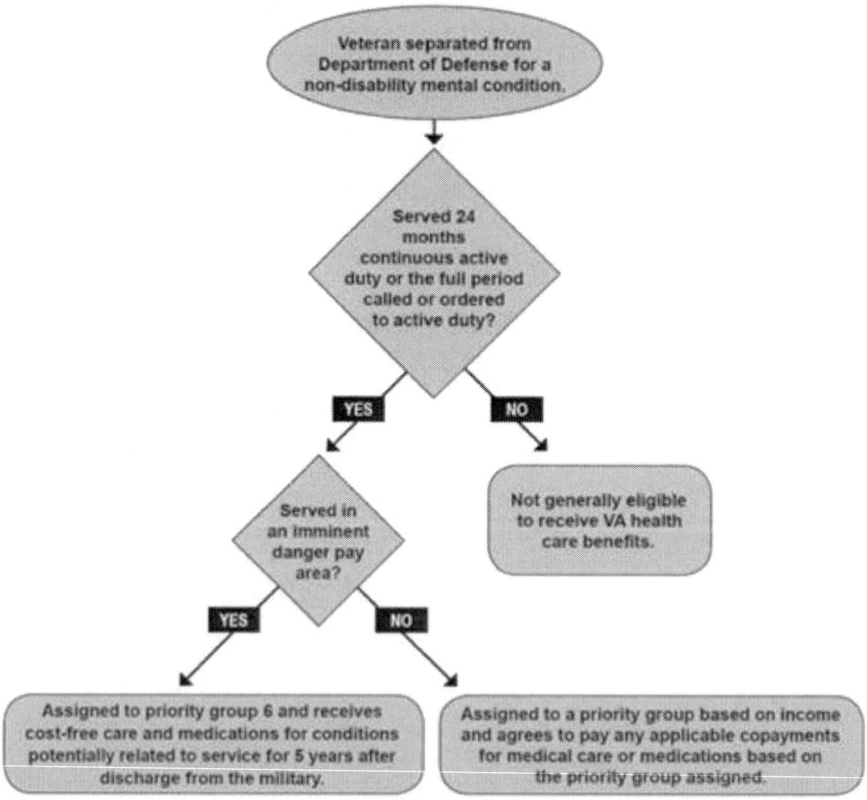

Source: GAO summary of VA information. | GAO-15-266.

Figure 1. Eligibility of Servicemembers Administratively Separated for Non-Disability Mental Conditions to Receive Health Care Benefits from the Department of Veterans Affairs (VA).

Once assigned a priority group and enrolled in VA's health care system, the veteran is eligible to receive VA's medical benefits package, which covers most of VA's medical services such as preventive care, and outpatient and inpatient diagnostic and treatment services, and includes services for mental health conditions.

End Notes

[1] Enlisted servicemembers are those in the active duty component and Reserve component—reservists and National Guard members. Officers may also be separated from the military; however, the separation process for officers is different from that of enlisted servicemembers and was not the focus of this review.

[2] We use "separation" to refer to administrative separations for non-disability mental conditions. DOD's requirements for these separations are in Department of Defense Instruction 1332.14 Enlisted Administrative Separations.

[3] These include mental conditions such as acute adjustment disorder, disruptive behavior disorder, impulse control disorder, personality disorder, and other mental conditions, such as attention-deficit hyperactivity disorder.

[4] GAO, Defense Health Care: Additional Efforts Needed to Ensure Compliance with Personality Disorder Separation Requirements, GAO-09-31 (Washington, D.C.: Oct. 31, 2008).

[5] Department of Defense Instruction 1336.01 Certificate of Release or Discharge from Active Duty (DD Form 214/5 Series) (Aug. 20, 2009).

[6] See GAO, Standards for Internal Control in the Federal Government, GAO/AIMD-00-21.3.1 (Washington, D.C.: November 1999).

[7] See GAO/AIMD-00-21.3.1.

[8] Servicemembers who choose to challenge the reason for their separations beyond 15 years after separation apply directly to the board for the correction of military records.

[9] According to DOD policy, servicemembers separated from the military for non-disability mental conditions receive a service characterization of honorable or general under honorable conditions.

[10] A separation code is a three letter code, with the last two letters indicating the condition for which the servicemember was separated, and the first letter indicating other information regarding the separation. In this report, when we refer to the separation code, we are referring to the information in the last two letters specifically.

[11] The other non-disability mental disorder category allows military services to group the four mental conditions listed above along with other conditions not assigned a specific code under one broad separation code.

[12] Examples of non-disability physical conditions for which servicemembers can be administratively separated include obesity and travel sickness.

[13] Department of Defense Instruction 1332.14 Enlisted Administrative Separations (Jan. 27, 2014). This DOD separation policy was the most current policy available at the time of our review. On December 4, 2014, DOD released an updated separation policy but this update did not affect the separation requirements discussed in this report.

[14] Servicemembers receive imminent danger pay (IDP) when they are on duty outside of the United States and are subject to the threat of physical harm or imminent danger due to

wartime conditions, terrorism, civil insurrection, or civil war. In some locations, IDP applies only for duty on the ground; and in other locations, ground, airspace, or duty aboard a ship at sea qualify.

[15] Based on DOD policy, an authorized mental health provider is a psychiatrist or clinical psychologist, a person with a doctorate in clinical social work, or a psychiatric nurse practitioner. In cases of outpatient mental health evaluations only, licensed clinical social workers who possess a master's degree in clinical social work will also be considered authorized mental health providers.

[16] See GAO/AIMD-00-21.3.1.

[17] While the Army, Navy, and Marine Corps use the broad code for most non-disability mental condition separations, these services also use the separation code specific to personality disorder. Army and Marine Corps officials stated that they use the personality disorder separation code because of DOD's interest in analyzing these types of separations. Navy officials could not explain why the Navy uses this code. The Navy and the Marine Corps use the personality disorder separation code for all personality disorder separations. The Army uses the personality disorder separation code for servicemembers that served less than 24 months; all other separations for personality disorder fall under the broad separation code "condition, not a disability." Army officials told us that they tried to discontinue using the personality disorder separation code in an effort to protect servicemembers from possible stigmatization of having a specific code that indicates a mental condition on the DD Form 214. However, according to Army officials, DOD officials told Army that it must use the specific code for personality disorder. In 2009, in response to DOD, Army continued using the personality disorder separation code for servicemembers that served less than 24 months, but began using the broader code of "condition, not a disability" for other servicemembers in an effort to protect those servicemembers who had served longer, according to Army officials.

[18] DOD officials stated that they have discussed adding the characterization of service to both copies of the DD Form 214 that the servicemember receives; however, no action has been taken.

[19] The Marine Corps was out of compliance with the requirement to notify the servicemember that the diagnosis of a personality disorder does not qualify as a disability (78 percent). Air Force was also out of compliance with this requirement (89 percent), as well as the requirement that the diagnosis be endorsed by the Air Force's Surgeon General (75 percent).

[20] The three requirements were (1) servicemember received formal counseling and was afforded the opportunity to improve behavior prior to being separated; (2) servicemember received written notification of impending separation based on personality disorder diagnosis; and (3) servicemember was advised that the diagnosis of a personality disorder does not qualify as a disability.

[21] The Marine Corps reported 90 percent compliance in its fiscal year 2008 report and 100 percent compliance in its fiscal year 2011 report.

[22] See GAO/AIMD-00-21.3.1.

[23] The Air Force provided Reserve and National Guard data in its fiscal year 2011 compliance report. The Air Force attempted to provide this information in its fiscal year 2012 report but noted problems identifying and assessing these two groups, and therefore, they were not included in that year's report. Otherwise, the services stated that they only included reservists or National Guard members in their reports if they were on active duty orders when they were separated for a personality disorder.

[24] Of the five reports submitted by each military service between fiscal years 2008 and 2012, the Army did not include this information in three reports, the Air Force did not include this information in one report, the Navy did not include this information in two reports, and the Marine Corps did not include this information in two reports.

[25] Navy officials could not explain to us why their reported numbers for a given fiscal year changed in subsequent reports and which numbers were correct. Army officials provided us with explanations as to why their reported numbers for a given fiscal year changed in subsequent reports. Army officials stated that the correct numbers are as follows: in fiscal year 2008 there were 641 personality disorder separations and in fiscal year 2009 there were 575 personality disorder separations.

[26] See GAO/AIMD-00-21.3.1.

[27] During our review, we found that the Air Force active duty separation policy [Air Force Instruction 36-3208 Administrative Separation of Airmen (July 2, 2013)] is not consistent with two of DOD's separation requirements. The Air Force policy does not require that servicemembers be assessed for PTSD or other mental illness co-morbidity prior to being separated for a non-disability mental condition, nor does it require servicemembers to be counseled in writing that such a diagnosis does not qualify as a disability. However, we found that these requirements are included in a checklist that is used by commanders and reviewed by a central personnel office during the separation process.

[28] Army Regulation 635-200 Personnel Separations Active Duty Enlisted Administrative Separations (Washington, D.C.: Sep. 6, 2011) and Army OTSG/MEDCOM Policy Memo 14-049 Administrative Separation of Soldiers for Personality Disorder (PD) under Chapters 5-13 and 5-17, or Other Designated Physical or Mental Conditions under Chapter 5-17 (Fort Sam Houston, T.X.: Jun. 23, 2014).

[29] The DOD requirement that the Army has not updated in its separation policy is that the servicemember must be counseled in writing that the diagnosis of a non-disability mental condition does not qualify as a disability.

[30] Army Regulation 135-178 Army National Guard and Army Reserve Enlisted Administrative Separations (Washington D.C.: Mar. 18, 2014).

[31] MILPERSMAN 1910-120 Separation by Reason of Convenience of the Government – Physical or Mental Conditions (Mar. 15, 2012). This policy applies to both active-duty and reserve servicemembers.

[32] Marine Corps Order 1900.16 Separation and Retirement Manual (Washington, D.C.: Nov. 26, 2013). According to Marine Corps officials, this policy applies to both active-duty and reserve servicemembers.

[33] Air Force Instruction 36-3209 Separation and Retirement Procedures for Air National Guard and Air Force Reserve Members (Washington D.C.: Apr. 14, 2005).

[34] Air Force officials told us that in order to separate a National Guard member for a non-disability mental condition, the commander would first have to notice that the National Guard member may have a non-disability mental condition and take action to get the member medically evaluated, before moving forward with that type of separation. The officials added that if a commander only sees a National Guard member once a month at drills, for example, they may not notice that the member may potentially have a non-disability mental condition; or if the National Guard member does not show up to drill, the commander would not notice such a condition and instead would likely separate the member for unsatisfactory duty performance.

[35] See GAO/AIMD-00-21.3.1.

[36] Air Force officials told us that National Guard members in initial active-duty training and those that have just returned from active-duty service in an IDP area may be separated for a non-disability mental condition. The officials stated that in these cases, the servicemembers would be on active-duty orders, and therefore, able to receive a medical evaluation from an Air Force medical provider. The officials added that if the provider diagnosed the servicemember with a non-disability mental condition that interfered with the performance of the servicemembers' military duties, the servicemember would be separated for a non-disability mental condition.

[37] The three requirements expanded were that non-disability mental condition diagnosis must (1) be corroborated by a peer- or higher-level mental health professional, (2) be endorsed by the military service's surgeon general; and (3) include an assessment to determine whether the servicemember has symptoms of PTSD or other mental illness co-morbidity.

[38] See GAO/AIMD-00-21.3.1.

[39] The Air Force, the Army, and the Navy each have a Judge Advocate General's (JAG) Corps that is composed of uniformed and civilian licensed attorneys. These attorneys provide legal advice to the command and staff, and represent servicemembers on military legal issues. The Marine Corps have a Judge Advocate Division where licensed attorneys provide advice on legal matters and oversee the Marine Corps legal community.

[40] For servicemembers that served in an IDP area, DOD requires that the servicemember's diagnosis be endorsed by the military service's surgeon general. According to officials, in order to fulfill this requirement, the Air Force central medical office, on behalf of the Air Force Surgeon General, reviews the separation packages of these servicemembers to see if all DOD separation requirements are met; whereas, the comparable medical offices in the Army and the Navy—which reviews medical information on behalf of the Marine Corps—review the separation packages of these servicemembers, but only to see if the DOD separation requirements that are medical in nature, such as the diagnosis addressing PTSD, have been met.

[41] According to Army officials, the National Guard JAG Corps does not generally review separation packages of National Guard members prior to their separation.

[42] Army officials also stated that they completed a review of the medical records of those servicemembers separated for all non-disability mental conditions from September 11, 2001, to August 31, 2012, to see if separation requirements that are medical in nature were met. However, officials could not provide the results of the review, or any related documentation, as the review has not yet been finalized and approved by the Army.

End Notes for Appendix I

[1] According to Department of Defense (DOD) policy, veterans separated from DOD for non-disability mental conditions receive a service characterization of honorable or general under honorable conditions.

[2] There are a number of exceptions to the minimum duty requirements that VA will determine once the veteran applies for VA health care benefits. 38 U.S.C. § 5303A.

[3] The number of veterans who can be enrolled in the health care program is dependent upon the amount of money VA receives in advance appropriations each year, 38 U.S.C. § 1710(a)(4). Since funds are limited, VA sets up priority groups to ensure that certain groups of veterans are able to be enrolled before others. The priority groups range from 1-8 with 1 being the

highest priority. Priority is generally based on service-connected disability, low income, and other recognized statuses such as former prisoners of war. 38 U.S.C. § 1705; 38 C.F.R. § 17.36.

[4] Veterans separated for non-disability mental conditions may be assigned to a higher priority group if, for example, they have other illnesses or injuries possibly related to their military service.

[5] Servicemembers receive imminent danger pay (IDP) when they are on duty outside of the United States and are subject to the threat of physical harm or imminent danger due to wartime conditions, terrorism, civil insurrection, or civil war. In some locations, IDP applies only for duty on the ground; and in other locations, ground, airspace, or duty aboard a ship at sea qualify.

[6] Currently enrolled veterans and new enrollees, who were discharged from active duty on or after January 28, 2003, are eligible for the enhanced benefits for 5 years post discharge. Veterans discharged from active duty before January 28, 2003, who applied for enrollment on or after January 28, 2008, were eligible for the enhanced benefit until January 28, 2011. 38 U.S.C. § 1710(e)(3).

[7] Unless otherwise exempted, veterans that served in an IDP area must either disclose their prior year gross household income or decline to provide their financial information and agree to make applicable copayments for care or services VA determines are clearly unrelated to their military service. This could include care or services for the non-disability mental condition for which the veteran was separated from the military since DOD and VA do not consider the condition to be service-related.

In: Service Members Separated ...
Editor: Scott Norton

ISBN: 978-1-63483-078-2

Chapter 2

DEFENSE HEALTH CARE: ADDITIONAL EFFORTS NEEDED TO ENSURE COMPLIANCE WITH PERSONALITY DISORDER SEPARATION REQUIREMENTS*

United States Government Accountability Office

ABBREVIATIONS

DMDC	Defense Manpower Data Center
DOD	Department of Defense
DSM	Diagnostic and Statistical Manual of Mental Disorders
OEF	Operation Enduring Freedom
OIF	Operation Iraqi Freedom
PTSD	post-traumatic stress disorder

WHY GAO DID THIS STUDY

At DOD, a personality disorder can render a servicemember unsuitable for service. GAO was required to report on personality disorder separations and

* This is an edited, reformatted and augmented version of The United States Government Accountability Office publication, GAO-09-31, dated October 2008.

examined (1) the extent that selected military installations complied with DOD's separation requirements and (2) how DOD ensures compliance with these requirements. GAO reviewed a sample of 312 servicemembers' records from four installations, representing the Army, Air Force, and Marine Corps, that had the highest or second highest number of Operation Enduring Freedom or Operation Iraqi Freedom servicemembers separated because of a personality disorder. The review is generalizable to the installations, but not to the services. GAO also reviewed 59 Navy servicemembers' records, but this review is not generalizable to the installation or the Navy because parts of the separation process could have been completed at multiple locations.

What GAO Recommends

GAO recommends that DOD (1) ensure that the services' personality disorder separations comply with DOD's requirements and (2) monitor the services' compliance. DOD concurred with GAO's first recommendation and partially concurred with the other. DOD stated that it will strengthen policy guidance for the services' compliance reporting, but stated that it is the responsibility of the services to ensure compliance. However, GAO's review indicates that reliance on the services is insufficient to ensure compliance.

What GAO Found

GAO's review of enlisted servicemembers' records found that the selected military installations GAO visited varied in their documented compliance with DOD's requirements for personality disorder separations. DOD has requirements for separations because of a personality disorder, which is defined as an enduring pattern of behavior that deviates markedly from expected behavior and has an onset in adolescence or early adulthood. The three key requirements established by DOD are that enlisted servicemembers (1) must be notified of their impending separation because of a personality disorder, (2) must be diagnosed with a personality disorder by a psychiatrist or psychologist who determines that servicemembers' personality disorder interferes with their ability to function in the military, and (3) must receive formal counseling about their problem with functioning in the military. For the four installations, compliance with the notification requirement was at or above 98 percent. The compliance rates for the requirement related to the personality disorder diagnosis ranged from 40 to 78 percent. For the requirement for formal counseling, compliance ranged from 40 to 99 percent. GAO's review of the documentation in the enlisted Navy servicemembers' records found that compliance varied by requirement. Ninety-five percent of enlisted Navy servicemembers' records had documentation indicating that enlisted servicemembers had been notified of their impending separation because of a personality disorder. Eighty-two percent had documentation that indicated compliance with the requirement that enlisted servicemembers must be diagnosed with a personality disorder by a psychiatrist or psychologist who determines that the personality disorder interferes with servicemembers' ability to function in the military. Seventy-seven percent had documentation indicating compliance with the requirement for formal counseling.

DOD does not have reasonable assurance that its key personality disorder separation requirements have been followed. DOD policy directs the military services to implement and ensure consistent administration of DOD's requirements for separating enlisted servicemembers because of a personality disorder. According to military service officials, the military services delegate to commanders with separation authority at military installations sole responsibility for ensuring that the separation requirements are followed for enlisted servicemembers under their command. When asked about the low rates of compliance for some of the separation requirements that GAO found, military officials responsible for reviewing the servicemembers' records with whom GAO spoke could not explain why these separations were approved if compliance with the separation requirements was not documented in the servicemembers' records. The military services have not established a way to determine whether the commanders with separation authority are ensuring that DOD's key separation requirements are met, and DOD does not have reasonable assurance that its requirements have been followed.

* * *

October 31, 2008

Congressional Addressees

The Department of Defense (DOD) requires that all servicemembers, including those who serve in Operation Enduring Freedom (OEF) and Operation Iraqi Freedom (OIF), be physically and psychologically suitable for military service.[1] Enlisted servicemembers who fail to meet this standard may be separated from the military.[2] One psychological condition that can render a servicemember unsuitable for military service is a personality disorder, which is defined as a long-standing, inflexible pattern of behavior that deviates markedly from expected behavior, has an onset in adolescence or early adulthood, and leads to distress or impairment.[3] Such a condition may make one unable to work within a military environment. DOD data show that from November 1, 2001, through June 30, 2007, about 26,000 enlisted servicemembers were separated from the military because of a personality disorder.[4] Of these 26,000, about 2,800 had deployed at least once in support of OEF/OIF.

Accurately diagnosing OEF/OIF servicemembers with a personality disorder can be challenging. Specifically, some of the symptoms of a personality disorder—irritability, feelings of detachment or estrangement from others, and aggressiveness—are similar to the symptoms of post-traumatic stress disorder (PTSD), a condition for which some OEF/OIF servicemembers may also be at risk. However, according to mental health experts and military mental health providers, one important difference between a personality disorder and PTSD is that a personality disorder is a long-standing condition, whereas PTSD is a condition that follows exposure to a traumatic event. Although servicemembers with personality disorders may have symptoms that first appear during their military duty, DOD does not consider this to be a condition caused by military service. A separation from the military because of a personality disorder can be stigmatizing and can have adverse consequences for servicemembers, such as limiting employment opportunities after servicemembers leave the military.

DOD has established three key requirements that the military services—Army, Air Force, Navy, and Marine Corps—must follow when separating enlisted servicemembers because of a personality disorder.[5] Specifically, before they are separated because of a personality disorder, enlisted servicemembers

- must receive notification of their impending separation because of a personality disorder;
- must receive, prior to the notification, a diagnosis of personality disorder by a psychiatrist or psychologist[6] who determines that the personality disorder interferes with servicemembers' ability to function in the military; and

- must receive formal counseling about their problem with functioning in the military.[7]

Typically, an enlisted servicemember's commander initiates the separation process. This commander, as well as a psychiatrist or psychologist, must follow the requirements established by DOD when separating a servicemember because of a personality disorder. Additionally, servicemembers undergoing the separation process have various protections available to them. For example, servicemembers may meet with a military attorney to discuss their rights during the separation process.

Congress included provisions in the National Defense Authorization Act for Fiscal Year 2008 that require us to review and report on OEF/OIF servicemembers' separations from military service because of a personality disorder,[8] and 11 senators also expressed interest in this work. For our review, we examined (1) the extent to which selected military installations complied with DOD requirements for separating enlisted servicemembers because of a personality disorder, (2) how DOD ensures compliance by the military services with personality disorder separation requirements, and (3) the extent to which enlisted servicemembers selected the protections available to them.

To determine the extent to which selected military installations[9] complied with DOD's personality disorder separation requirements, we reviewed DOD and the military services' separation regulations and instructions to identify the key requirements for separating enlisted servicemembers because of a personality disorder. We included only enlisted servicemembers because officers generally are able to resign at any time rather than be involuntarily separated. We obtained DOD data for enlisted OEF/OIF servicemembers separated because of a personality disorder from November 1, 2001, through June 30, 2007, which we determined to be sufficiently reliable for our purposes by corroborating these data with information in the servicemembers' personnel records. We analyzed these data to determine which installations across the military services had the highest number of enlisted OEF/OIF servicemembers separated because of a personality disorder. We selected four installations to visit—Fort Carson (Army), Fort Hood (Army), Davis-Monthan Air Force Base (Air Force), and Camp Pendleton (Marine Corps)—because these installations accounted for the highest or second highest number of enlisted OEF/OIF servicemembers separated because of a personality disorder from November 1, 2001, through June 30, 2007, among their military service's installations.[10,11] For three of the installations we visited, we obtained and reviewed personnel records for a random sample of enlisted servicemembers whose certificates of release[12] indicated that they were separated from these installations because of a personality disorder. For the fourth installation, we obtained and reviewed personnel records for all of the enlisted servicemembers whose certificates of release indicated that they were separated from that installation because of a personality disorder. We reviewed all of these enlisted servicemembers' records because the total number of servicemembers separated from this installation was too small to draw a random, generalizable sample. Our findings based on our compliance review can be generalized to each of the four installations but cannot be generalized to the military services.

In addition to the four military installations from the Army, Air Force, and Marine Corps, we visited Naval Base San Diego. We obtained and reviewed personnel records for enlisted Navy servicemembers whose certificates of release indicated that they were separated because of a personality disorder. During the course of our review, Navy officials at this base told us that enlisted Navy servicemembers selected for our review were transferred to the transient personnel unit at Naval Base San Diego from a Navy ship at various points in the separation process.[13] According to a Navy official, most enlisted Navy servicemembers were diagnosed, formally counseled, and notified of their impending separation while on board a Navy ship and were transferred to the transient personnel unit at Naval Base San Diego to receive their certificates of release. Other enlisted Navy servicemembers were diagnosed, formally counseled, and notified of their impending separation while at Naval Base San Diego. We could not generalize our findings to Naval Base San Diego because some of the elements of the separation process could have been completed while these servicemembers were on board a Navy ship. We also could not generalize to the Navy. Therefore, we have reported the results of our review of enlisted Navy servicemembers' records separately from our presentation of findings based on our review of the other four military installations.

For our compliance review, we examined 312 personnel records for enlisted servicemembers from the Army, Air Force, and Marine Corps installations and 59 records for enlisted servicemembers from the Navy— 371 records in total. We obtained these records from each military service's central repository, where the personnel records of servicemembers who have been separated from the military are stored. In each of these records, we reviewed what is known as a separation packet, which is required to contain documents related to a servicemember's separation.[14] According to military service officials responsible for the separation policy, the separation packet is required to include documentation demonstrating that DOD's three key requirements for a personality disorder separation have been met.

To complete our compliance review, we reviewed servicemembers' separation packets first to see if the packets contained documentation that servicemembers had been notified of their impending separation because of a personality disorder. If the servicemembers' separation packets lacked such documentation, we did not assess compliance for the other two key separation requirements. If the packets did include such documentation, we reviewed the packets to determine whether they contained documentation required by the military services demonstrating that the other two key requirements had been met. Table 1 describes the criteria we used to determine compliance.

Table 1. Criteria to Determine Compliance from Review of Separation Packets in Enlisted Servicemembers' Personnel Records

Requirement	Compliance	Noncompliance
Servicemembers must be notified of the separation because of a personality disorder	Separation packet contained a notification letter of the separation because of a personality disorder	Separation packet did not contain a notification letter of the separation because of a personality disorder
Servicemembers must receive a personality disorder diagnosis by a psychiatrist or psychologist who determines that the personality disorder interferes with servicemembers' ability to function in the military	Separation packet contained what is known as a medical form that documents the following three parts of this requirement: (a) A diagnosis of personality disorder (b) Made by psychiatrist or psychologist (c) Who determines that the personality disorder interferes with servicemembers' ability to function in the military	Separation packet did not contain a medical form or Separation packet included a medical form, but documentation supporting one or more of the following parts of this requirement was missing or was incorrect: (a) A diagnosis of personality disorder (b) Made by psychiatrist or psychologist (c) Who determines that the personality disorder interferes with servicemembers' ability to function in the military
Servicemembers must be formally counseled about their problem with functioning in the military	Separation packet contained a counseling form	Separation packet did not include a counseling form

Source: GAO analysis of DOD's and military services' separation regulations and instructions.

To determine how DOD ensures compliance with its personality disorder separation requirements by the military services, we reviewed DOD regulations and interviewed officials from DOD and the military services. To determine the extent to which enlisted servicemembers selected the protections available to them, such as consulting legal counsel prior to being separated, we reviewed the same 371 enlisted servicemembers' separation packets as we reviewed to determine compliance with DOD's personality disorder separation requirements—312 separation packets for enlisted servicemembers from the Army, Air Force, and Marine Corps installations and 59 separation packets for enlisted servicemembers from the Navy.[15] For the 371 enlisted servicemembers whose separation packets we reviewed, we also obtained information from the military services to determine whether any of these servicemembers appealed the reason for their separation. Appendix I provides more detailed information on our methodology. We conducted this performance audit from May 2007 through August 2008 in accordance with generally accepted government auditing standards. Those standards require that we plan and perform the audit to obtain sufficient, appropriate evidence to provide a reasonable basis for our findings and conclusions based on our audit objectives. We believe that the evidence obtained provides a reasonable basis for our findings and conclusions based on our audit objectives.

RESULTS IN BRIEF

The four military installations we visited varied in their compliance with DOD's three key requirements for personality disorder separations. For the four installations, compliance with the requirement to notify enlisted servicemembers of their impending separation because of a personality disorder was at or above 98 percent. The compliance rates for the requirement that enlisted servicemembers must be diagnosed with a personality disorder by a psychiatrist or psychologist who determines that the personality disorder interferes with servicemembers' ability to function in the military ranged from 40 to 78 percent. For the requirement that enlisted servicemembers be formally counseled about their problem with functioning in the military, compliance ranged from 40 to 99 percent. Our review of the documentation in the enlisted Navy servicemembers' separation packets found that compliance varied by requirement. Ninety-five percent of enlisted Navy servicemembers' separation packets had documentation indicating that they had been notified of their impending separation because of a personality disorder. Eighty-two percent had documentation that indicated compliance with the requirement that enlisted servicemembers must be diagnosed with a personality disorder by a psychiatrist or psychologist who determines that the personality disorder interferes with servicemembers' ability to function in the military. Seventy-seven percent had documentation indicating compliance with the requirement for formal counseling.

DOD does not have reasonable assurance that its key personality disorder separation requirements have been followed. DOD policy directs the military services to implement and ensure consistent administration of DOD's requirements for separating enlisted servicemembers because of a personality disorder. In turn, according to officials in each of the military services, the military services delegate to commanders with separation authority at military installations sole responsibility for ensuring that the key separation requirements are followed for enlisted servicemembers under their command. When asked about the low rates of compliance for some of the separation requirements that we found, the military officials responsible for reviewing the separation packets with whom we spoke could not explain why these separations were approved if compliance with the separation requirements was not documented in the servicemembers' separation packets. The military services have given commanders with separation authority sole responsibility for ensuring compliance with DOD's requirements, but the military services have not established a way to determine whether these commanders are ensuring that DOD's key separation requirements are met. Furthermore, DOD does not have reasonable assurance that its requirements for separating enlisted servicemembers because of a personality disorder have been followed.

The extent to which enlisted servicemembers from the four installations selected the protections available to them varied. For example, the majority of enlisted servicemembers—about 93 percent—requested copies of the separation documents, while few enlisted servicemembers— 12 percent—indicated that they wanted to submit statements on their own behalf to the commander with separation authority. Among enlisted Navy servicemembers, 66 percent requested copies of their separation documents, while 5 percent stated that they wanted to submit statements on their own behalf to the commander with separation authority. After separation had occurred, three enlisted servicemembers from the four installations we visited and among enlisted Navy servicemembers whose separation packets we reviewed chose to challenge the reason for their separation.

To help ensure that DOD's requirements for personality disorder separations are met and to help increase assurance that these separations are appropriate, we recommend that the Secretary of Defense direct the Under Secretary of Defense for Personnel and Readiness to (1) direct the Secretaries of the Army, the Air Force, and the Navy and the Commandant of the Marine Corps to develop a system to ensure that personality disorder separations are conducted in accordance with DOD's requirements and (2) ensure that DOD monitors the military services' compliance with DOD's personality disorder separation requirements. In written comments on a draft of this report, DOD concurred with our recommendation that the military services develop a system to ensure that personality disorder separations be conducted in accordance with DOD's requirements. DOD partially concurred with our recommendation that DOD monitor the military services' compliance with DOD's personality disorder separation requirements. DOD stated that it will strengthen policy guidance related to the military services' standardized compliance reporting, but that it is the responsibility of the military services to ensure compliance with DOD policy. However, as we stated in our draft report, DOD's reliance on the military services to ensure compliance with its separation requirements does not provide reasonable assurance that these requirements will be followed. The low rates of compliance we found for some of DOD's key personality disorder separation requirements suggest the need for another system to ensure compliance with these requirements, as well as the need for DOD to monitor the military services' compliance. DOD also provided technical comments, which we incorporated as appropriate.

BACKGROUND

Enlisted servicemembers can be separated from the military when they are found to be unsuitable for continued military service. According to DOD regulations, enlisted servicemembers can be separated for reasons such as misconduct, failure to overcome substance abuse, and certain mental health conditions, including a personality disorder. A personality disorder by itself does not make enlisted servicemembers unsuitable for military service. DOD requires that the disorder be severe enough that it interferes with an enlisted servicemember's ability to function in the military.[16]

DOD and the military services require that to diagnose a personality disorder a psychiatrist or psychologist use criteria established in the *Diagnostic and Statistical Manual of Mental Disorders* (DSM), which was developed by the American Psychiatric Association.[17] Similarly, in the private sector, clinicians use criteria in the DSM to diagnose a personality disorder, but in some instances, clinicians other than psychiatrists or psychologists, such as licensed clinical social workers, may make this diagnosis.

Diagnosing a personality disorder in a servicemember who has served in combat can be complicated by the fact that some symptoms of a personality disorder may be similar to symptoms of combat-related mental health conditions. For example, both personality disorder and PTSD have similar symptoms of feelings of detachment or estrangement from others, and irritability. According to the American Psychiatric Association and the American Psychological Association, the only way to distinguish a personality disorder from a combat-related mental health condition, such as PTSD, is by getting an in-depth medical and personal history from the servicemember that is corroborated, if possible, by family and friends.

According to DOD officials, the three key requirements that the military services must follow when separating an enlisted servicemember are designed to help ensure that enlisted servicemembers are separated for the appropriate reason.[18,19] Documentation of compliance with these requirements is to be included in the separation packet found in the enlisted servicemember's personnel record, as required by the military services. The separation packet is required to contain other documents related to the enlisted servicemember's separation. According to officials from the military services, the servicemember's immediate commander gives the separation packet to an installation official who is to review the packet to verify that the requirements for the personality disorder separation have been met. If this review verifies that the requirements have been met, the separation packet is then sent to a commander at the installation who has authority for approving a personality disorder separation for that enlisted servicemember. This commander is a higher-level officer than the enlisted servicemember's immediate commander. A military installation may have more than one commander who has the authority to approve separations because of a personality disorder. However, each commander with separation authority approves separations only for enlisted servicemembers under his or her command.

Once enlisted servicemembers have been separated from military service, they receive certificates of release from the military, which include information on the reason for separation and an official characterization of their time in the service.[20] For enlisted servicemembers separated because of a personality disorder, their certificates of release would state that the reason for their separation was a personality disorder. Employers may request to see separated servicemembers' certificates of release to verify their military service, and employers may make employment decisions based on the information they see on servicemembers' certificates of release.

Enlisted servicemembers have protections available to them when going through the separation process. All enlisted servicemembers can submit statements on their own behalf to the commander with separation authority, consult with legal counsel prior to separation, and obtain copies of the separation packet that is sent to the commander with separation authority. In addition, enlisted servicemembers with 6 or more years of military service are eligible to request a hearing before an administrative board.[21] An administrative board hearing allows enlisted servicemembers to have legal representation, call witnesses, and speak on their own behalf in defending against the recommended separation. The board includes at least three members who, following a hearing, make a recommendation to the commander with separation authority as to whether the enlisted servicemember should be separated.

Enlisted servicemembers also have protections available to them after they have been separated. They may challenge the reasons given for their separations after they have been separated from the military. Within 15 years after separation from the military, enlisted servicemembers may appeal their separation to a discharge review board. Further, enlisted servicemembers may appeal the discharge review board's decision by applying to a board for the correction of military records.[22]

SELECTED MILITARY INSTALLATIONS' COMPLIANCE WITH THREE KEY PERSONALITY DISORDER SEPARATION REQUIREMENTS VARIED

The four military installations we visited varied in their compliance with DOD's three key requirements for personality disorder separations. For the four installations, compliance with the first requirement—to notify enlisted servicemembers of their impending separation because of a personality disorder—was at or above 98 percent. For the second requirement, that enlisted servicemembers must be diagnosed with a personality disorder by a psychiatrist or psychologist who determines that the personality disorder interferes with servicemembers' ability to function in the military, the compliance rates ranged from 40 to 78 percent. Compliance ranged from 40 to 99 percent for the third requirement, that enlisted servicemembers receive formal counseling about their problem with functioning in the military. Our review of the documentation in the enlisted Navy servicemembers' separation packets found that compliance varied by requirement.

Compliance with the Notification Requirement Ranged from 98 to 100 Percent

Across the four installations, the percentage of enlisted servicemembers' separation packets that documented compliance with the notification requirement ranged from 98 to 100 percent. Of the 312 enlisted servicemembers' separation packets included in our review, only 4 did not contain documentation that the servicemembers received notification that they were being separated because of a personality disorder. We did not assess whether the separation packets for these 4 servicemembers had documentation that indicated compliance for the remaining two key separation requirements.

Compliance with the Requirement Related to the Personality Disorder Diagnosis Ranged from 40 to 78 Percent

Across the four installations, the percentage of enlisted servicemembers' separation packets that had documentation indicating compliance with all three parts of the second requirement—that enlisted servicemembers separated because of a personality disorder (1) be diagnosed with a personality disorder (2) by a psychiatrist or psychologist who (3) determines that the personality disorder interferes with servicemembers' ability to function in the military—ranged from 40 to 78 percent. Noncompliance with this requirement occurred in two ways: enlisted servicemembers' separation packets did not contain the medical form used to document the three parts of this requirement or servicemembers' separation packets contained the medical form but documentation on the form for one or more of the three parts of this requirement was missing or incorrect. Figure 1 summarizes the four installations' compliance rates for this requirement.

We found that 34 enlisted servicemembers' separation packets did not contain a medical form, which is used to document compliance with the three parts of this requirement. We also found that of the enlisted servicemembers' separation packets that contained a medical form, the medical form in 66 of these packets did not contain information needed to fulfill all three parts of the requirement.

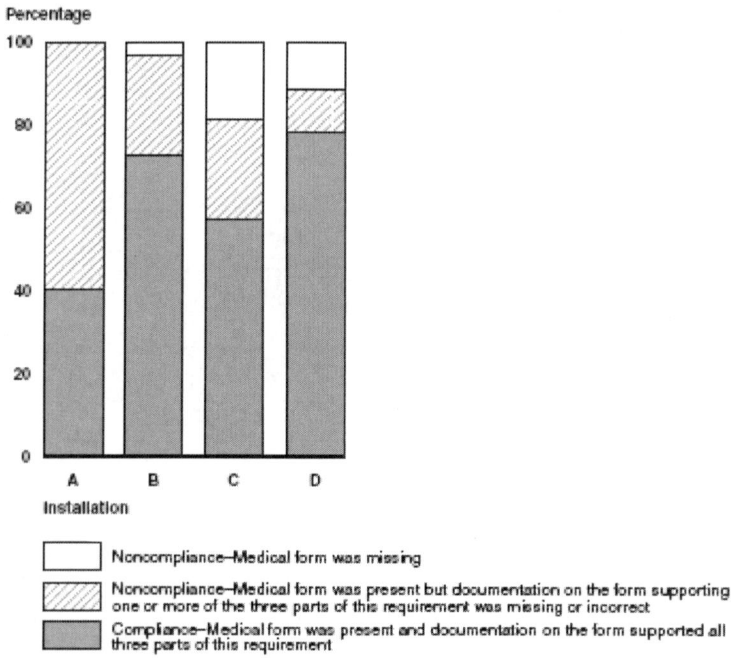

Source: GAO analysis of enlisted servicemembers' personnel records obtained from the military services.

Notes: We determined compliance with this requirement by reviewing 308 personnel records of enlisted servicemembers whose separation packets had documentation that they had been notified of their impending separation because of a personality disorder.

Air Force officials acknowledged that prior to October 2006 some enlisted servicemembers with a mental health diagnosis other than a personality disorder, such as adjustment disorder, were erroneously separated under the reason of a personality disorder. However in October 2006, Air Force officials stated that they took steps to correct this error. Some of the servicemembers separated from the Air Force installation we visited may have been affected by this error.

Figure 1. Rate of Documented Compliance at Selected Military Installations with Requirement That Enlisted Servicemembers Be Diagnosed with a Personality Disorder by a Psychiatrist or Psychologist Who Determines That the Personality Disorder Interferes with Servicemembers' Ability to Function in the Military, for Separations Completed from November 1, 2001, through June 30, 2007.

For example, 27 of these 66 enlisted servicemembers' medical forms had documentation indicating that the servicemember had been diagnosed with a personality disorder, but there was also information in the medical form indicating that the diagnosis was not made by a psychiatrist or psychologist. In some of these cases, we found that the diagnosis of a personality disorder was made by a licensed clinical social worker or other type of provider, such as a battalion surgeon.

Compliance with the Requirement for Formal Counseling Ranged from 40 to 99 Percent

We found that compliance with the requirement that enlisted servicemembers receive formal counseling about their problem with functioning in the military ranged from 40 to 99 percent.[23] Across the four installations, we found that 42 enlisted servicemembers' separation packets did not contain a counseling form documenting that servicemembers received formal counseling as required. As a result, these 42 servicemembers' separation packets were noncompliant with this requirement. Figure 2 summarizes the four installations' compliance rates for this requirement.

Documented Compliance with the Three Key Personality Disorder Separation Requirements Varied for Enlisted Navy Servicemembers' Separation Packets That We Reviewed

Our review of the documentation in 59 enlisted Navy servicemembers' separation packets found that compliance varied by requirement. Of the separation packets that we reviewed, 95 percent had documentation indicating that enlisted servicemembers had been notified of their impending separation because of a personality disorder. (Three enlisted servicemembers' separation packets did not contain documentation of this requirement, and as a result, we did not assess compliance with the remaining two requirements for these three servicemembers' separation packets.) The requirement that enlisted servicemembers be diagnosed with a personality disorder by a psychiatrist or psychologist who determines that the personality disorder interferes with servicemembers' ability to function in the military had a compliance rate of 82 percent for the 56 remaining enlisted Navy servicemembers' separation packets that we reviewed.

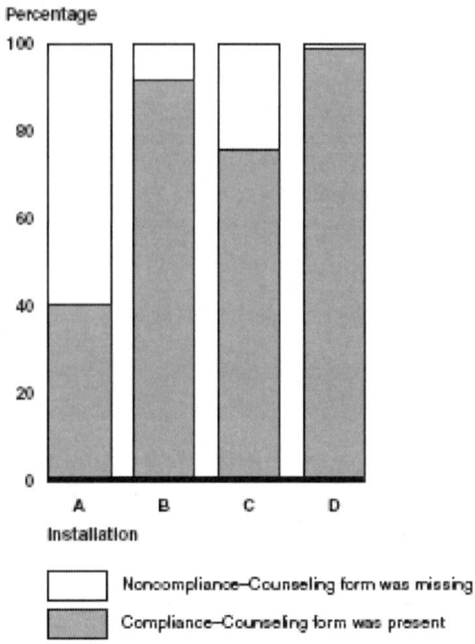

Source: GAO analysis of enlisted servicemembers' personnel records obtained from the military services.

Note: We determined compliance with this requirement by reviewing 308 personnel records of enlisted servicemembers whose separation packets had documentation that they had been notified of their impending separation because of a personality disorder.

Figure 2. Rate of Documented Compliance at Selected Military Installations with Requirement That Enlisted Servicemembers Receive Formal Counseling about Their Problem with Functioning in the Military, for Separations Completed from November 1, 2001, through June 30, 2007.

Of the 56, we found that 1 enlisted Navy servicemember's separation packet did not contain a medical form, which is used to document compliance with the three parts of this requirement. We also found that 9 of the 56 enlisted Navy servicemembers' separation packets contained a medical form, but did not have documentation indicating compliance with all three parts of this requirement. Most of these—6—did not have documentation indicating that the diagnosis of a personality disorder was made by a psychiatrist or psychologist. For the requirement for formal counseling, 77 percent of the 56 enlisted Navy servicemembers' separation packets contained documentation that enlisted servicemembers received formal counseling about their problem with functioning in the military.[24]

DOD Does Not Have Reasonable Assurance That Its Separation Requirements Have Been Followed

DOD does not have reasonable assurance that its key personality disorder separation requirements have been followed. DOD policy directs the military services to implement and ensure consistent administration of DOD's requirements for separating enlisted servicemembers because of a personality disorder. In turn, according to officials in each of the military services, the military services delegate to commanders with separation authority at the military installations sole responsibility for ensuring that the requirements are followed for enlisted servicemembers under their command.

According to military officials at the installations we visited, to ensure compliance with DOD's key separation requirements, the commander with separation authority has an official at the installation examine the enlisted servicemember's separation packet prior to the separation to determine that all requirements have been met. Military officials responsible for reviewing the separation packets at the installations we visited explained that when the official who is reviewing the separation packet discovers that a requirement for separation has not been documented, the reviewing official is supposed to take steps to resolve the situation. For example, if the official reviewing the separation packets does not find documentation that enlisted servicemembers have been formally counseled about their problem with functioning in the military, the reviewing official would verify that the formal counseling had occurred and then obtain documentation of that counseling session. Similarly, a Navy legal official told us that enlisted servicemembers' separation packets should be reviewed to make sure that DOD's key separation requirements have been met before the separations are approved. When we asked about the low rates of compliance for some of the separation requirements that we found at the Army, Air Force, and Marine Corps installations we visited and for the enlisted Navy servicemembers' records that we reviewed, the military officials responsible for reviewing the separation packets with whom we spoke could not explain why these separations were approved if compliance with the separation requirements was not documented in the separation packet.

Having given sole responsibility to the commanders with separation authority to ensure compliance, the military services have not established a way to determine whether these commanders are ensuring that DOD's key requirements are met. Furthermore, DOD does not have reasonable assurance that its requirements for separating enlisted servicemembers because of a personality disorder have been followed.

Enlisted Servicemembers' Selection of Protections Available During and after Separation Varied

At the four installations we visited, enlisted servicemembers who were separated because of a personality disorder varied in the extent to which they selected the protections available to them during the separation process, depending on the specific protection. Based on our review of separation packets in the enlisted servicemembers' personnel records, we found that a small proportion of enlisted servicemembers - 12 percent - stated that they wanted to submit statements on their own behalf to the commander with separation authority. Of these servicemembers who submitted a statement, 18 percent submitted a statement that either questioned whether the diagnosis of a personality disorder was an accurate diagnosis or requested not to be separated. All of these servicemembers were separated. We also found that 38 percent of enlisted servicemembers at the installations we visited stated that they wanted to consult with legal counsel prior to their separation. According to legal officials at the installations we visited, enlisted servicemembers may seek legal counsel to discuss the implications of a personality disorder separation, seek advice on how to stay in the military, or obtain information on their eligibility for Department of Veterans Affairs' benefits, such as health and educational benefits, after separation. For enlisted Navy servicemembers whose separation packets we reviewed, 5 percent selected to submit statements and 5 percent selected to consult with counsel prior to separation.

Based on our review of enlisted servicemembers' separation packets for the installations we visited, we found that the majority of servicemembers requested copies of their separation packets, which are sent to the commander with separation authority. Specifically, 289 of 312 enlisted servicemembers in our review at the four installations - 93 percent - requested copies of their separation packets, while 66 percent of enlisted Navy servicemembers in our review requested copies of their separation packets. We also found that no enlisted servicemembers—either at the installations we visited or among the enlisted Navy servicemembers whose separation packets we reviewed - requested a hearing before an administrative board prior to their separation.[25]

Enlisted servicemembers may challenge the reason given for their separation to a discharge review board after the separation has been completed. For the four installations we visited and for enlisted Navy servicemembers, we found that three enlisted servicemembers applied to their military service's discharge review board to challenge the reason for their separation. Of these three, one servicemember received a change to the reason for separation because the discharge review board found that the separation because of a personality disorder was unjust. For this servicemember, the reason for separation was changed from personality disorder to the reason of secretarial authority of that military service.[26] The other two servicemembers who applied for a change to their reason for separation did not receive a change because the discharge review board found that the documentation present in the personnel record supported the personality disorder separation. The two servicemembers who were unsuccessful in their appeal to the discharge review board did not choose to appeal the discharge review board's decision to the board for the correction of military records.

CONCLUSION

DOD has established requirements that are intended to help ensure that enlisted servicemembers separated because of a personality disorder are separated appropriately. Failure to comply with these requirements increases the risk of enlisted servicemembers being inappropriately separated because of a personality disorder. For enlisted servicemembers, the stakes are high because a personality disorder separation can carry a long-term stigma in the civilian world. Because DOD relies on the military services to ensure compliance with its key personality disorder separation requirements, and because the military services rely solely on commanders with separation authority to ensure compliance with these requirements, there is a lack of reasonable assurance that the requirements have been met. During our review of enlisted servicemembers' separation packets at the four military installations and for enlisted Navy servicemembers' separation packets we reviewed, the low rates of compliance we found for some of the key personality disorder separation requirements indicate that the military services need a system, beyond relying on the commanders who are making separation decisions, to ensure compliance with DOD's personality disorder separation requirements. Additionally, DOD needs to monitor the military services' compliance with these requirements. Until this happens, DOD does not have reasonable assurance that personality disorder separations of enlisted servicemembers have been appropriate.

Recommendations for Executive Action

To help ensure that DOD's requirements for personality disorder separations are met and to help increase assurance that these separations are appropriate, we recommend that the Secretary of Defense direct the Under Secretary of Defense for Personnel and Readiness to

1. direct the Secretaries of the Army, the Air Force, and the Navy and the Commandant of the Marine Corps to develop a system to ensure that personality disorder separations are conducted in accordance with DOD's requirements and
2. ensure that DOD monitors the military services' compliance with DOD's personality disorder separation requirements.

Agency Comments and Our Evaluation

In written comments on a draft of this report, DOD concurred with our recommendation that the military services develop a system to ensure that personality disorder separations are conducted in accordance with DOD's requirements. DOD partially concurred with our recommendation that DOD monitor the military services' compliance with DOD's personality disorder separation requirements. DOD stated that it will strengthen policy guidance related to the military services' standardized compliance reporting, but that it is the responsibility of the military services to ensure compliance with DOD policy. However, as we stated in our draft report, DOD's reliance on the military services to ensure compliance with its separation requirements has not provided reasonable assurance that these requirements will be followed. We believe that the low rates of compliance we found for some of DOD's key personality disorder separation requirements suggest the need for another system to ensure compliance with these requirements, as well as the need for DOD to monitor the military services' compliance.

DOD suggested that we change the title of our draft report to indicate that our subject area was personnel management and not defense health care. We have not changed the title. For an enlisted servicemember to be separated because of a personality disorder, the servicemember must first be diagnosed as having a personality disorder. Therefore, we consider our review of DOD's separation process for servicemembers with personality disorders a review of a health care issue.

In its comments, DOD also identified two inaccuracies in our description of DOD's separation requirements. DOD pointed out that its policy does not state that a servicemember's written notification of the impending separation has to come from a servicemember's commander, as we indicated in our draft report. According to DOD, the policy does not specify who must provide this written notification. We revised our draft report to clarify our discussion of this requirement. However, this change did not affect the results of our compliance review because we determined compliance based on whether servicemembers' separation packets contained a notification letter and not on who notified the servicemember. DOD also pointed out that its policy does not state that servicemembers must receive formal counseling from their supervisors about their problem with functioning in the military, as we stated in our draft report. According to DOD, the policy does not state who should provide the formal counseling to the servicemember; however, we were told by a DOD separation policy official that the counseling should be done by the servicemember's supervisor. We revised our draft report to clarify our discussion of this requirement. This also did not change the results of our compliance review because we assessed compliance based on whether servicemembers' separation packets contained a counseling form and not on who counseled the servicemember.

DOD also provided technical comments, which we incorporated as appropriate.

Randall B. Williamson
Director, Health Care

APPENDIX I: SCOPE AND METHODOLOGY

To meet our objectives, we examined Department of Defense (DOD) separation regulations that the military services are required to follow to help ensure that enlisted servicemembers are separated for the appropriate reasons. For our review, we examined (1) the extent to which selected military installations complied with DOD requirements for separating enlisted servicemembers because of a personality disorder, (2) how DOD ensures compliance with personality disorder separation requirements by the military services, and (3) the extent to which enlisted servicemembers who are separated because of a personality disorder selected protections available to them.

For this review, we included enlisted servicemembers from the Army, Air Force, Navy, and Marine Corps. We included only enlisted servicemembers because officers are able to resign at any time rather than be involuntarily separated. We included enlisted servicemembers who deployed at least once in support of Operation Enduring Freedom (OEF) or Operation Iraqi Freedom (OIF). The Coast Guard was excluded because it is under the direction of the Department of Homeland Security and represents a very small portion of servicemembers deployed in support of OEF and OIF. For this review, enlisted servicemembers are those in the active duty component and Reserve component—reservists and National Guard members—who were discharged or released from active duty from November 1, 2001—the first full month of combat operations for OEF— through June 30, 2007—the latest date for which data were available from DOD at the time of our review.

We obtained data from DOD's Defense Manpower Data Center (DMDC) on the number of enlisted servicemembers who had been separated from the military because of a personality disorder from November 1, 2001, through June 30, 2007. These data came from DMDC's Active Duty Military Personnel Transaction File and DMDC's Reserve Components Common Personnel Data Transaction File, which are databases that contain servicemember-level data, such as Social Security number, education level, date of birth, pay grade, separation program designator code, and reenlistment eligibility. The Active Duty Military Personnel Transaction File contains a transaction record for every individual entrance, separation, or reenlistment in the Army, Air Force, Navy, and Marine Corps within a specific time frame. The Reserve Components Common Personnel Data Transaction File contains this information for every individual entrance, separation, or reenlistment in the Army National Guard, Army Reserve, Air National Guard, Air Force Reserve, Navy Reserve, and Marine Corps Reserve within a specific time frame. We also asked that DMDC indicate, from its Contingency Tracking System Deployment File, if any enlisted servicemembers who were separated because of a personality disorder were also deployed, for at least one tour of duty, in support of OEF or OIF. The Contingency Tracking System Deployment File is a database that includes data elements for all servicemembers deployed in support of OEF/OIF. A contingency tracking system deployment is defined as a servicemember being physically located within the OEF or OIF combat zones/areas of operation, or specifically identified by the military service as directly supporting the OEF/OIF mission outside of the designated combat zone. We determined that the DMDC data were sufficiently reliable because we corroborated these data with information in the enlisted servicemembers' personnel records.

Based on our analysis of the data provided by DMDC, we selected four military installations across the Army, Air Force, and Marine Corps to visit based on whether the installation had the highest or second highest number of enlisted OEF/OIF servicemembers separated because of a personality disorder for that service. We selected one installation each from the Air Force and the Marine Corps. We selected two Army installations because at the time of our review, the Army had the majority of servicemembers deployed in support of OEF/OIF when compared with the Air Force and the Marine Corps. Among Marine Corps installations, we selected Camp Pendleton, in California, which had the second highest number of enlisted servicemembers separated because of a personality disorder during this time period. This installation was selected because the Marine Corps installation with the highest number of enlisted servicemembers separated because of a personality disorder was in the midst of a deployment cycle and requested that we not visit. The other military installations we selected were Fort Carson (Army), Colorado; Fort Hood (Army), Texas; and Davis-Monthan Air Force Base (Air Force), Arizona.

In addition to the four military installations we visited, we visited Naval Base San Diego. We selected Naval Base San Diego based on DMDC's data, which identified this naval base as having the second highest number of enlisted OEF/OIF Navy servicemembers separated because of a personality disorder from November 1, 2001, through June 30, 2007.[1]

During the course of our review, Navy officials at this base told us that enlisted Navy servicemembers selected for our review were transferred to the transient personnel unit at Naval Base San Diego from a Navy ship at various points in the separation process.[2] According to a Navy official, most enlisted Navy servicemembers were diagnosed, formally counseled, and notified of their impending separation while on board a Navy ship and were transferred to the transient personnel unit at Naval Base San Diego to receive their certificates of release. Other enlisted Navy servicemembers were diagnosed, formally counseled, and notified of their impending separation while at Naval Base San Diego. We could not generalize our findings to Naval Base San Diego because some of the elements of the separation process could have been completed while these servicemembers were on board a Navy ship. Therefore, we have reported the results of our review of enlisted Navy servicemembers' records separately from our presentation of findings based on our review of the other four military installations.

To determine the extent to which the four military installations and enlisted Navy servicemembers' records that we reviewed complied with DOD personality disorder separation requirements, we reviewed DOD's and the military services' enlisted administrative separation regulations and instructions to identify the key requirements for separating enlisted servicemembers because of a personality disorder. We also interviewed officials at each of the military services' headquarters who are responsible for overseeing separation policy. We interviewed additional officials at each of the four selected installations and at Naval Base San Diego, including mental health providers, staff judge advocates, legal counsel with defense services, unit commanders, administrators of the Medical Evaluation Board, and officials in the transition/separation offices, to understand the administrative separation process.

Additionally, to determine whether the selected installations and enlisted Navy servicemembers' records that we reviewed complied with DOD's requirements for separating servicemembers because of a personality disorder, we obtained and reviewed the personnel records of selected servicemembers to verify that their certificates of release indicated that they were separated because of a personality disorder. We obtained these records from each military service's central repository, where the personnel records of servicemembers who have been separated from the military are stored. According to military service officials responsible for separation policy, the separation packet, which is found in the enlisted servicemember's personnel record, is required to contain documents related to the separation, including documents indicating that DOD's three key requirements have been met.[3]

For three of the installations we selected, we reviewed the personnel records of a random, generalizable sample of enlisted servicemembers who deployed at least once in support of OEF/OIF and who were separated from that installation because of a personality disorder from November 1, 2001, through June 30, 2007. For the other installation we selected, we reviewed the personnel records of all enlisted servicemembers who deployed at least once in support of OEF/OIF and who were separated from that installation because of a personality disorder from November 1, 2001, through June 30, 2007, because the number of servicemembers separated from that installation was too small to draw a random, generalizable sample. In total, we included 343 enlisted servicemembers' personnel records across the four installations. Of these 343 records, 312 enlisted servicemembers' personnel records were included in our documentation review because their personnel records contained separation packets, which we needed to review to determine compliance. Of the 31 servicemembers' personnel records that were excluded from our review, 3 had separation packets that were illegible. The remaining 28 servicemembers' personnel records did not have separation packets available for our review.

We also obtained 94 enlisted Navy servicemembers' personnel records from the Navy's central repository, where the personnel records of servicemembers who have been separated are stored after they leave the Navy. We reviewed the personnel records of all enlisted Navy servicemembers who deployed at least once in support of OEF/OIF and who were separated from Naval Base San Diego because of a personality disorder from November 1, 2001, through June 30, 2007, because the number of enlisted servicemembers separated from Naval Base San Diego was too small to draw a random, generalizable sample. We reviewed these personnel records to determine if they contained separation packets, which are required by the Navy. Of the 94 enlisted Navy servicemembers, 59 servicemembers' personnel records were included in our review because their records contained separation packets, which were needed for us to determine compliance. We excluded 35 enlisted Navy servicemembers' personnel records from our evaluation of compliance. One enlisted servicemember's separation packet was illegible and 34 enlisted servicemembers' separation packets were not available for review.

In our review, we determined compliance for each of the three key personality disorder separation requirements by reviewing the documentation in the enlisted servicemembers' separation packets to see if it indicated compliance with that requirement. If the enlisted servicemember's separation packet did not include documentation that the servicemember had been notified of the impending separation because of a personality disorder—one of the key requirements for a personality disorder separation—we did not assess compliance with the other two key requirements. Table 2 describes the criteria we used to determine compliance.

Our review of compliance can be generalized to each of the four installations we visited, but not to the military services. For enlisted Navy servicemembers whose separation packets we reviewed, we cannot generalize to Naval Base San Diego or to the Navy.

Table 2. Criteria to Determine Compliance from Review of Separation Packets in Enlisted Servicemembers' Personnel Records

Requirement	Compliance	Noncompliance
Servicemembers must be notified of the separation because of a personality disorder	Separation packet contained a notification letter of the separation because of a personality disorder	Separation packet did not contain a notification letter of the separation because of a personality disorder
Servicemembers must receive a personality disorder diagnosis by a psychiatrist or psychologist who determines that the personality disorder interferes with servicemembers' ability to function in the military	Separation packet contained what is known as a medical form that documents the following three parts of this requirement: (a) A diagnosis of personality disorder (b) Made by psychiatrist or psychologist (c) Who determines that the personality disorder interferes with servicemembers' ability to function in the military	Separation packet did not contain a medical form or Separation packet included a medical form, but documentation supporting one or more of the following parts of this requirement was missing or was incorrect: (a) A diagnosis of personality disorder (b) Made by psychiatrist or psychologist (c) Who determines that the personality disorder interferes with servicemembers' ability to function in the military
Servicemembers must be formally counseled about their problem with functioning in the military	Separation packet contained a counseling form	Separation packet did not include a counseling form

Source: GAO analysis of DOD's and military services' separation regulations and instructions.

To determine how DOD ensures compliance by the military services with requirements for separating enlisted servicemembers because of a personality disorder, we reviewed DOD regulations and interviewed DOD and the military services' officials responsible for separation policy. Additionally, we interviewed military officials responsible for legal services at the installations we visited and at Naval Base San Diego about how they ensure compliance with DOD's key requirements for personality disorder separations.

INDEX

A

adjustment, 8, 25, 44
administrators, 54
adulthood, 5, 32, 34
Afghanistan, 8
agencies, 6
Air Force, 3, 4, 11, 13, 14, 16, 17, 18, 19, 21, 22, 26, 27, 28, 32, 34, 35, 36, 38, 40, 44, 47, 50, 52, 53, 57, 58
American Psychiatric Association, 40, 41, 57
American Psychological Association, 41
annual review, 19
appropriations, 28
assessment, 9, 18, 28
audit, 6, 38, 57
authority, 33, 39, 41, 42, 47, 48, 49, 59

B

benefits, 4, 5, 23, 25, 28, 29, 48

C

category a, 25
certificate, 7, 58
civil war, 10, 26, 29
Coast Guard, 52
community, 28
compensation, 4
compliance, 2, 3, 6, 12, 13, 14, 15, 16, 19, 20, 21, 22, 26, 32, 33, 35, 36, 37, 38, 39, 40, 41, 42, 43, 44, 45, 46, 47, 49, 50, 51, 52, 55, 56, 57, 59
consulting, 38
contingency, 52
counsel, 38, 42, 48, 54
counseling, 26, 32, 35, 37, 39, 43, 45, 46, 47, 51, 56, 58, 59

D

danger, 1, 8, 9, 10, 23, 25, 29
deficiencies, 6, 8, 9, 14
deficit, 25
Department of Defense (DOD), vii, 1, 2, 3, 4, 5, 6, 7, 8, 9, 10, 11, 12, 13, 14, 15, 16, 17, 18, 19, 20, 21, 22, 25, 26, 27, 28, 29, 31, 32, 33, 34, 35, 37, 38, 39, 40, 41, 42, 47, 49, 50, 51, 52, 54, 56, 57, 58, 59
Department of Homeland Security, 52
Diagnostic and Statistical Manual of Mental Disorders, 31, 40, 57
directives, 6
disability, vii, 2, 3, 4, 5, 6, 7, 8, 9, 10, 11, 12, 13, 17, 18, 19, 20, 21, 22, 23, 25, 26, 27, 28, 29

disorder, 5, 6, 8, 9, 13, 25, 26, 27, 31, 32, 33, 34, 35, 37, 38, 39, 40, 41, 42, 43, 44, 45, 47, 48, 49, 50, 51, 52, 53, 54, 55, 56, 57, 58
distress, 5, 34
draft, 22, 40, 50, 51
DSM, 40

E

education, 52
employers, 3, 11, 12, 42
employment, 34, 42
employment opportunities, 34
enrollment, 23, 29
estrangement, 34, 41

F

federal government, 16, 25
fiscal year 2009, 13, 16, 27
Fort Hood, 35, 53
funding, 18
funds, 28

G

GAO, 1, 2, 3, 5, 10, 16, 24, 25, 26, 27, 28, 31, 32, 33, 37, 44, 46, 56
guidance, 32, 40, 50

H

health, 5, 10, 18, 23, 24, 25, 26, 28, 34, 41, 48, 50, 58
health care, 23, 24, 25, 28, 50
health care system, 24, 25
health condition, 41
House of Representatives, 4
household income, 24, 29
hyperactivity, 25

I

identification, 21
imminent danger pay (IDP), 1, 8, 9, 10, 13, 14, 17, 19, 20, 23, 24, 25, 28, 29
inspections, 20
Iraq, 8
irritability, 34, 41

J

Judge Advocate General (JAG), 1, 19, 28

L

legal issues, 28

M

majority, 39, 48, 53, 58
management, 6, 50
Marine Corps, 2, 4, 10, 11, 13, 14, 15, 16, 17, 20, 21, 22, 26, 27, 28, 32, 34, 35, 36, 38, 40, 47, 50, 52, 53, 57, 58, 59
media, 11
medical, 17, 23, 25, 28, 37, 41, 43, 45, 46, 56
mental disorder, 8, 25
mental health, 8, 9, 10, 18, 25, 26, 28, 34, 40, 41, 44, 54, 58
mental illness, 9, 10, 27, 28
methodology, 38
military service, vii, 2, 3, 4, 5, 6, 7, 8, 9, 10, 11, 12, 13, 14, 15, 17, 19, 20, 21, 22, 23, 25, 27, 28, 29, 33, 34, 35, 36, 37, 38, 39, 40, 41, 42, 44, 46, 47, 49, 50, 51, 53, 54, 56, 57, 58, 59
morbidity, 9, 10, 27, 28

N

National Defense Authorization Act, 1, 5, 35
Non-disability mental conditions, vii, 2

O

obesity, 2, 25
officials, 2, 3, 5, 6, 11, 13, 14, 15, 17, 18, 19, 20, 26, 27, 28, 33, 36, 38, 39, 41, 44, 47, 48, 53, 54, 56
Operation Enduring Freedom, 5, 31, 32, 33, 52
Operation Iraqi Freedom, 5, 31, 32, 33, 52
operations, 6, 14, 16, 19, 52
outpatient, 10, 25, 26
oversight, 3, 5, 6, 12, 16, 19, 20, 22

P

personal history, 41
personality disorder, vii, 2, 3, 5, 6, 8, 9, 10, 12, 13, 14, 15, 16, 19, 20, 25, 26, 27, 31, 32, 33, 34, 35, 36, 37, 38, 39, 40, 41, 42, 43, 44, 45, 46, 47, 48, 49, 50, 51, 52, 53, 54, 55, 56, 57, 58, 59
post-traumatic stress disorder (PTSD), 1, 4, 9, 10, 20, 27, 28, 31, 34, 41
prisoners of war, 29
private sector, 40
protection, 48, 58
psychiatrist, 9, 10, 26, 32, 34, 35, 37, 38, 40, 42, 43, 45, 46, 56, 59
psychologist, 9, 10, 26, 32, 35, 37, 38, 40, 42, 43, 45, 46, 56, 59

R

regulations, 22, 35, 37, 38, 40, 51, 54, 56
requirements, vii, 2, 3, 4, 5, 6, 8, 9, 10, 12, 13, 14, 15, 17, 18, 19, 20, 21, 22, 23, 25, 26, 27, 28, 32, 33, 34, 35, 37, 38, 39, 41, 42, 43, 45, 47, 49, 50, 51, 54, 55, 56, 57, 58
resolution, 6
response, 12, 26
risk, 18, 20, 21, 34, 49

S

Secretary of Defense, 21, 22, 40, 50
Senate, 4
September 11, 28
servicemember, vii
services, vii, 2, 3, 4, 5, 6, 8, 10, 11, 12, 13, 14, 15, 17, 19, 20, 21, 22, 25, 26, 29, 32, 33, 34, 35, 37, 38, 39, 40, 41, 44, 46, 47, 49, 50, 51, 54, 56, 58
single test, 58
Social Security, 52
social workers, 10, 26, 41
stakeholders, 3, 12
state(s), 3, 6, 14, 15, 16, 19, 41, 51, 59
stigma, 11, 49
substance abuse, 40
supervisor(s), 51, 58
symptoms, 9, 28, 34, 41

T

technical comments, 23, 40, 51
terrorism, 10, 26, 29
time frame, 52
training, 28
transactions, 3, 6, 11, 18
treatment, 25

U

uniform, 21, 22

W

waiver, 59